CW01312644

Take the Time

Travel Memoirs
from Around the World

Richard Boudreau

Copyright © 2023

All rights reserved.
No part of this publication may be reproduced, distributed, or transmitted in any form or by any means, including photocopying, recording, or other electronic or mechanical methods, without the prior written permission of the publisher, except in the case of brief quotations embodied in reviews and certain other non-commercial uses permitted by copyright law.

ISBN 9798861100861

FIRST EDITION

Printed in the United States of America

CONTENTS

An Easter Service to Remember.. 1
Around the World in Sixty Days 9
In Search of a Priest in Bolivia.. 16
The Bird Who Wanted a Cracker 22
Eight Years in Mexico Without a Visa....................................... 29
Buying an Emerald in Phnom Penh... 35
Two Nights in Dhaka.. 43
Phosphorescence at Three in the Morning 49
Diving Off a Boat in Ha Long Bay 54
A Shoeshine at the Golden Temple 59
The Turtles of San Agustinillo 65
Where is Sibu?.. 71
Adventures at Bako National Park... 76
The Biggest Flowers in the World.. 81
Waving to a Policeman 84
Free Camping in New Zealand 90
A Flight Over the Nazca Lines 94
Don't Eat the Lettuce 98
The Mysterious Tea 103

The Stolen Camera	107
The Best Snorkeling	111
The Energy of Machu Picchu	115
Pishing for Birds	120
Five Weeks in Patzcuaro	124
Dengue Fever	128
Ninety-Three and Still Traveling	132
A Nail in the Door	135
The Ring that Changed Color	140
Popcorn and Potatoes	144
The Orphanage of Trujillo	148
A Map for Saul	152
The Killings at Todos Santos	158
The Love Motel in Vera Cruz	164
Driving Up the River	167
Thirty Minutes Late for a Quetzal	173
An Earthquake in Southern Mexico	179
The Apartment Has a Pizza Oven	183
An Airplane Ride from Merida to Oaxaca	187
Ice Cream and Levitation	192
Teaching Koreans in Guatemala	197
A River Runs Through Our Kitchen	201
One Hundred Ten Countries After Sixty-Two	206
Emu Oil	210

The Brown Rice of Lombok 215
The Hole in the Road 220
Two Paintings for a Lipstick 226
A Day on the Irrawaddy 231
A Tibetan Monk in Southern India 236
A Protein Feast for Ten Dollars 241
Tri Binh One 245
Spotting Rhinos in Nepal 250
Mount Everest for Christmas 255
A Picnic on the Great Wall 260
An Apartment in Thailand 264
How We Did It 269

INTRODUCTION

By Sean Boudreau

Twenty-three years ago, my wife and I asked my father, Richard, to say a blessing at our wedding. This year, as we watched the video and *really* listened to his words, I realized that he had tried to pass on the richness of what he has learned in life—the immense value in taking the time to enjoy the gifts of this world. The stories in this book tell of the unique adventures that he and his wife, Christine, experienced and treasured in their extensive travels.

> As we gather together on this wedding day,
>
> let us ask God to give you
>
> the time to listen to the birds,
>
> the time to listen to the waves,
>
> and the time to listen to the wind.
>
> Take the time to be still,
>
> and the time to be silent.
>
> I urge you to take the time in your marriage
>
> to allow God to fill you with deep peace and deep love.
>
> With these things, you will experience
>
> a touch of heaven right here on earth.

CHAPTER 1

An Easter Service to Remember

It was a hot sunny day as we cruised up the Rajang River of Borneo. The crowded boat was making its way from Sibu, a port city in the state of Sarawak, to the small river town of Kapit. Two hours upstream, it made a three-minute stop at the town of Song. Here, we disembarked, hoping to find overnight lodging and passage to the Nanga Bangkit Longhouse the next morning.

Song was nothing but a four-block town with a few waterfront shops and two guesthouses. We quickly found a small comfortable room, put down our backpacks and set off to find transport for the four-hour boat journey up the Rajang tributary, the Katibas River. Somewhere along the banks of the river would be our destination, a secluded longhouse without the trimmings of western civilization.

"Christine, did you notice there are no westerners in this town?" I asked.

"There were none on the boat either," she commented with enthusiasm.

"It's great, isn't it?"

We always try to get away from the tourist trail as much as possible, and it appeared that this time, we had accomplished that objective. Tourist towns have advantages in that they provide the comforts of nicer accommodations, western restaurants, and a host of other creature comforts. However, to get a real feel for a culture, we usually try to find an area or village away from the well-worn touristy areas, in hopes of developing an appreciation for the local inhabitants. This venture to a far-off longhouse, was designed to do just that for us in Borneo.

Tourists generally went from Sibu to Kapit and then on to Belaga, bypassing Song. Belaga is a tourist town known for gift shops, hotels, western restaurants, and bars—exactly what we wanted to avoid this time around.

We had asked Susan, our Kuching friend, about a Dayak longhouse that would be away from the growth and civilization that was overtaking this part of Malaysia. She said she knew the perfect one and advised us to practice our sign language, as they wouldn't speak any English.

"Once in Song," she told us, "Ask around for a powered canoe that can transport you up the Katibas. Ask the Chinese; they should speak English. And don't worry, there are no longer any head hunters."

We went out to the dock, and sure enough, a shop owner told us "Ask for Chinaman with small boat in morning."

"What time?" Christine asked.

"Maybe six o'clock, maybe six-thirty," he instructed.

That evening, we had dinner at one of a series of open-air restaurants in the center of town. Each stall offered a variation of Sarawak food. The basic ingredients seemed to be rice, fish, chicken, and local spinach. The fish or chicken could be found in soups, grilled or barbequed. An assortment of homemade sweets was available for dessert. We enjoyed our food, though we appeared to be a point of curiosity among the townspeople. After concluding our meal, we took a brief walk around town and settled in for a good night's rest.

We knew 5 a.m. would come quickly and had no idea what comforts would be afforded us the following evening.

The next morning, we found the Chinese-Malayan with no difficulty and were off by 6:30 with three other Dayak passengers in the twenty-foot motorized canoe. The boat had a canopy, for which the need became apparent three hours upstream.

Dayaks are a group of local tribes that inhabit portions of Sarawak State in eastern Borneo. Although they were once known as ferocious warriors and headhunters, they are now very peaceful. Many reside around larger cities like the capital, Kuching, while others live off the land within the thick tropical jungles. Our goal was to visit a group living in the hinterland, beyond the reach of most travelers.

The *Sungei Katibas* as locals call it, was raging during this rainy season and it progressively got rougher and narrower as we proceeded upriver. Occasionally, we passed encampments and longhouses, but they were few and far between. There appeared to be very little commerce on the river, as we passed no other riverboats. Evidently, the river inhabitants live by hunting, fishing, and rice production. Occasionally, young men hire out as contract laborers for the large lumber companies. We met several young men employed by lumber conglomerates who had worked as far away as the Amazon jungles of Brazil. The need to travel that far for work surprised us, as the remains of an active lumber industry were everywhere. The forests of this part of Borneo were being cut while we were there, regardless of what the government proclaimed.

After about three hours, the rain began. It came down in buckets. We were extremely thankful for the boat's canopy, as ten seconds out in one of these downpours would have us completely drenched.

Nanga Bangkit was a forty-eight-door longhouse sitting high up the banks of the Katibas, completely surrounded by jungle. A few children stood by the path leading up to the longhouse, but understandably, there were few people out during the rainstorm.

Normally, it is advisable to make arrangements in advance when visiting Dayaks, but that was impossible at Nanga Bangkit because of its distance from civilization; there were no means of communication. We decided to wait until somebody approached us. Being uninvited guests, we thought it would be unwise to enter their place without some sort of invitation.

"Let's get under the eve of this outbuilding and we'll see what happens," I suggested to Christine.

"Good idea," she responded, as we rushed to the shed.

At this point, I should explain that a longhouse is a village in itself. Here, there were forty-eight families living within one massive structure. The families each live in their own area, which is a condo-type unit with privacy, subdivided into kitchen, bedrooms, and living area. All of the units are linked by one huge enclosed porch. This area runs the length of the longhouse, which in this case was well over one thousand feet long. The porch area is open from one end to the other so families can visit one another without going outdoors. This is a particularly nice feature during the monsoons. It is like having an entire village under one roof with consideration for privacy.

After standing under the eve for a few minutes, an elderly lady came out, looked at us, and with pity in her eyes, she waved us in. She directed us to sit on the floor of this massive porch as she went off. She had not spoken a word to us, so we assumed she didn't speak English and possibly did not have the authority to extend invitations beyond entering the porch. We were very appreciative for her help in getting us out of the rain, and eagerly awaited her next move.

A few children and adults peered at us from a distance, but nobody spoke a word. After five or ten minutes, a middle-aged man came over with several of his friends. He looked us over and asked, "Speak English?"

"Yes," I responded.

"Where from?"

"The United States and Christine is from England."

"RC?" he asked.

I looked at Christine, "What is RC?"

"RC could mean Roman Catholic," she suggested. "I'll ask."

"RC is Roman Catholic?"

"Yes."

In truth, I told them that I was Roman Catholic and it brought broad smiles to their faces. With the ice broken, he said, "You want eat?"

"Yes," we responded, and within a few minutes, we were immersed in a delicious meal consisting of venison, rice, and jungle fiddleheads. As we ate, more and more of the inhabitants gathered to watch the fair-skinned foreigners.

The afternoon proceeded slowly as lack of a common language hampered conversation. Sign language was the best we could manage at this stage, until another middle-aged man joined us. He had traveled to the logging camps of the Amazon and spoke some English. We soon discovered that he was the chief's brother. He informed us that the chief would be in later to meet with us. We had advance notice from our friend in Kuching that little would occur in any

Dayak longhouse without the chief's presence, so we were eager to meet with him.

As yet, we did not have a place to stay the night, but felt increasingly confident, as the people were very friendly. We were hopeful the chief would allow us to stay the night. Our comfort that evening depended entirely on the chief, for if he did not invite us to remain, we had no alternative but to spend the night on the banks of the river. There were no boats traversing in any direction at this point in the mid-afternoon.

After about an hour, three men approached with a logbook in hand. Our friend, Susan, had told us that it would be necessary to sign a logbook in order to stay the night, so we saw this as another positive sign. The men sat down opposite us. The one with the logbook wrote "2003" on the cover and handed it over to me while opening to page one.

To our astonishment, the page was blank. In fact, the entire book was blank. We were both surprised and pleased that we were the only visitors this year. This being the day before Easter meant the village had not had a guest, western or Malay, for at least four months.

Christine looked at me excitedly with a smile. "We could be the first guests in a year, or even longer, who knows?"

After another hour, the chief arrived and spoke enough English to invite us into his lodging and offered for us to stay the night. Needless to say, we responded affirmatively and were delighted with his hospitality. He was very friendly, yet business-like, always seeing to our needs in a punctual manner. This middle-aged man was considered young to be a chief, as most were elderly. His business acumen was evidently what won him the election.

"Can come to RC ceremony tonight?" he asked.

"Yes!" we both responded.

The remainder of the afternoon and early evening were spent talking in English and sign language to the children of the chief and his extended family. We taught them some English and they taught us some Dayak words. It was a lot of fun and we had a wonderful time with the kids. Children throughout the world always seem friendlier and more eager to learn than adults. Possibly, they are simply less inhibited.

After sharing an excellent meal with the family, the village-head asked us to join the other members of the longhouse in the Easter religious service. We followed him and his family to the center of the longhouse porch, where we sat in a circle on the floor with the members of the congregation. We pretended to listen attentively, though we could not understand a word that the deacon spoke.

A priest from Sibu visits once or twice per year to say a mass, so the village relies on its partially trained cleric. I later learned that the priest had visited Sibu for a weekend, during which time, the deacon was trained for his religious duties. Other than the visits by the priest, this man was on his own.

As the service progressed, we noticed a young black and white cat sitting under the table that the deacon was using to support his book. The feline itself was not unusual, as there were many pets around the village. Cats, dogs, and chickens seemed to meander about freely.

Everything changed though, as a rhinoceros beetle came crashing down from the open rafters into the center of the circle of people. Before anybody could blink an eye, the cat trounced on the stymied beetle with the ferocity of a lion attacking its prey. Needless to say, the congregation was distracted from its religious service. Eventually, an elderly lady came to the rescue of the beetle, escorting it, dead or alive, out the door on a piece of board.

Christine looked at me and whispered, "An Easter service to be remembered."

After the rituals were over, we enjoyed homemade rice wine with the deacon and a group of the villagers. Although conversation was limited, we had a pleasant time and were enthralled with the hospitality.

As the night progressed, we were escorted to the chief's residence, where we were provided a mattress on the living room floor. In spite of the various jungle noises, we slept well. The uncertainty of the day as well as the challenge of communicating with non-English speakers had worn us out. There had been more anxiety to the adventure than we had anticipated.

At 5:30 the next morning, the chief woke us. After a light breakfast, we accompanied him on his motorized canoe and he brought us down the river to Song. Fortunately, it did not rain on this voyage, as his boat did not have a canopy. As an added bonus, we enjoyed some bird watching as we descended the rapids of the Katibas.

Since that episode in Nanga Bangkit, we have often discussed how challenging it must have been for early explorers and missionaries to communicate with natives of various parts of the world. Without a common spoken language and sole reliance on sign language, it can be quite difficult and tiring. Being face to face with such a different culture than our own was not easy, but was truly an extraordinary experience.

CHAPTER 2

Around the World in Sixty Days

Bagan is a magnificent archeological site in central Burma (Myanmar). We were standing on top of one of its highest temples, watching the brilliant sunrise over hundreds of other pagodas with mountains in the far distance. The ancient monuments, over two thousand of them, hint at what must have been a great civilization. At 6 a.m., the sky was bright red, the start of what would be a hot April day. The places of worship are set astride of the Irrawaddy River, a major transportation route that runs through the center of the nation from north to south.

Over the next few hours, we would be transported from temple to temple via horse and cart. Some temples were small and ornately adorned, while others were huge with beautiful golden Buddhas within. There was an enormous variety regarding both size and complexity.

Some thirteen hundred years ago, the wealthy people of Burma would have pagodas built in their honor in hopes of seeing a better afterlife, sort of like buying your way into heaven. Presumably, it was a major expense to have such a grand edifice erected. Small temples are often ten to fifteen feet high, while large pagodas are upwards of fifty feet. The entire complex has hundreds of temples, all on this one flat plain covering several thousand acres.

Christine and I felt like we were at one of those special places on earth, one that is endowed with religious mysticism.

The immensity of it all was awe-inspiring.

By ten that morning, it was so hot that the horse and buggy driver took us back to our guesthouse for breakfast and a midday rest in our air-conditioned room. This was one of the few places in Burma that had electricity twenty-four hours a day. It accommodated tourists, and their money, of which the country has too little of each. Nevertheless, it was nice having air conditioning as April is the hottest month of the year in Southeast Asia. We had been warned in advance to take a slow pace, in anticipation of the heat. The split day worked out well for us. We expected to spend a full month in Burma, so we had an extra day here and there if needed. There was no need for us to rush in the heat. With an early morning and late afternoon schedule, we were able to take in all of the major temples in a few days without exhausting ourselves or suffering heat stroke.

At four in the afternoon, our driver picked us up and we were off to see more of the archeological sites. At sunset, we found ourselves at another high temple. It overlooked the Irrawaddy to the west, with the setting sun behind the river. The sky was cloudless on this particular evening and the sun, a huge red ball. The scene felt made-to-order and we relished every moment.

We spent four days on this schedule before feeling we had seen enough of the sites to satisfy our curiosity and interest, though we anticipate returning to Bagan again. There is still much that we have not seen and some sites that we would like to revisit. Over the course of our travels, we have found that there are certain times when one suffers from over exposure. At such a time, we prefer to move on and hopefully return at another date. Four days at Bagan with its April heat had taken its toll on us.

The next day, we bused east for eight hours to the town of Kalaw. This small hill town is cooler and much more comfortable. Here we would relax by walking around town, enjoying the morning market, which seemed endless with its colorful array of fruits, vegetables, clothing, and numerous household items. The market did not sell any paintings, craft goods, or gifts, as the town saw very few visitors. It was one of those places that people drove by en route to Inle Lake, seldom stopping. We were delighted to have stayed, as it provided us the opportunity to see an aspect of Burma which is often not experienced by travelers.

It was interesting to note that many of the shopkeepers and restaurant owners in town were of Indian descent. Their families had been here since the days of British colonization. They had been brought to this nation in supervisory capacities to oversee logging operations and stayed on when the English left. Kalaw was visited by the British administrators and their Indian subordinates because of its lower temperatures, which made for pleasant getaways.

At a beautiful monastery overlooking the city, we met a Korean Buddhist monk who was studying in Burma on a six-month visa. She spoke English and provided us with a guided tour of the monastery and temple. We noted that six-month visas were available to monks, while the best we could get was twenty-eight days. The military dictatorship, in spite of many atrocities, still allows people their religion, which is refreshing. Throughout our travels in Burma, we had no indication the inhabitants were prohibited from practicing Buddhism, which is the principal religion of the nation. In fact, we found many people frequenting the temples we visited.

After two days in Kalaw, we planned to take a pickup truck, the standard means of transportation for the locals, for the two-hour ride to Inle Lake. We hesitated though, when we saw the jam-packed truck. The driver smiled at us and directed Christine to squeeze in front and had me sit on the roof rack with our two backpacks. Fortunately, the road was good, which is not always the case in Burma. With the exception of one brief downpour, it was a rather pleasant journey. Needless to say, by journey's end, I was not alone on the roof. We had picked up many more passengers along the way. The enterprising driver earned as much as he could.

By the time we arrived at Inle Lake, it was late afternoon. We immediately found our way to a small, one-story guesthouse. It was quiet, comfortable, and had a ceiling fan. Because of its elevation, the lake area is usually quite pleasant with a light breeze blowing over the valley.

After a brief rest, we began to stroll into the town center in search of a restaurant. With the exception of a rare motorbike, there was little to no traffic which made for relaxed walking. Suddenly, we heard a boisterous "Hello!" As we turned, another, "Hello, where are you from?"

"I'm Richard and this is Christine," I responded to the westerners, as they approached.

"I'm Henry and this is Martha," the sixty-year-old-looking man stated as he extended his hand and went on to say, "We're going around the world. What are you doing here?"

"We just arrived," Christine responded. "We're hoping to see the Inle Lake area over the next week or so."

"We heard of a nice little restaurant that serves good western food," he said. "Shall we have a go at it together?"

We answered affirmatively, as we usually find it informative to dine or simply chat with other travelers. They often have been someplace we are going to or would like to see at some point. We have found fellow travelers to be excellent sources of information regarding nice, clean restaurants and guesthouses, as well as information about transportation systems. The facts that they can provide are usually much more current than guidebooks. We also enjoy listening to others' travel tales and commiserating with compatriots.

We arrived at the small burger restaurant and even though this type of place would not have been our first choice, we thought the company would be interesting, a small sacrifice to pay for what could bring helpful information from people in the midst of circumnavigating the globe.

"We're from New York and have taken sixty days off to go around the world. How about you?" Henry proudly proclaimed as we sat down.

"I'm originally from England and Richard is originally from Massachusetts," Christine told them. "But at present, we travel nearly year-round."

Martha seemed interested, but Henry continued, "We started from New York and flew to London, then on to Paris, then Rome, then Delhi, India."

I quickly interjected, "We were in India this year. What places did you visit?"

"We saw the Taj, spent a day in Delhi, then we had to fly to Bangkok for a couple of days, and now Burma," Henry answered without taking a breath.

"It sounds like a busy schedule," Christine commented while looking at Martha.

Undaunted, Henry announced, "We want to see it all!"

We saw the weary look in Martha's eyes as she listened to Henry. She interjected, "If I hold up that long…"

Henry kept going, "We enjoyed Rangoon, with its beautiful stupa on the hill, and even got to the market." Then as if he were just getting started, he added, "We then flew to Mandalay to see the puppet show."

We were beginning to realize Henry and Martha were going to many places but exploring very little. We had found one week too short for Mandalay, yet it sounded like these folks had only stayed for one or two days. I wondered how long they had spent in Bagan, if they had managed Mandalay in two days.

"How did you like Bagan?" I asked.

"Where?" he asked.

"Bagan," I responded, "the archeological site on the Irrawaddy."

"Never heard of it. Did you say it was in Burma?" he questioned.

Christine and I looked at each other, acknowledging we had little to learn from Henry. Going to Burma and not seeing Bagan is like going to Rome and not seeing Saint Peter's. Henry and Martha could tell their friends they had been to Burma, but in fact, they had seen very little of what that precious country has to offer. It's understandable that certain sites may not appeal to everyone, but with him never even hearing of Bagan, it seemed as though they hadn't read any background on the country. Even the slightest research would have enlightened them about this gem of an area.

Martha and Henry would go around the world in sixty days and get a glimpse at a number of places, but with that haste, they were not able to enjoy spectacular sites that were right before their eyes. Additionally, for Martha, her exhaustion made the situation even worse. At this stage of their travels, she seemed to be just going through the motions. With appropriate time, they could have stopped for a rest along the way to re-energize themselves.

As we were finishing dinner, Henry asked, "Where are you going next?"

I told him that we planned to spend the next five months seeing more of Southeast Asia and then we would fly back to the States.

"Did you fly over the Atlantic to get to India?" he asked.

"Yes," Christine responded.

"And will you fly east, over the Pacific to get back home?"

"We will."

Henry then extended his hand and said, "Congratulations, you too are going around the world."

Martha and Henry flew out of the Inle Lake area the next morning. They had only spent one night. They would complete their circumnavigation within the allotted sixty days, as planned, and be proud of their accomplishment.

As for Christine and I, we continued at our slower pace, enjoying Inle Lake and its environs over the next week. The lovely people of Burma had much to offer and we intended to stay the twenty-eight days that our visa allowed in order to take in as much of the country as possible.

Although we learned little from Martha and Henry in regards to specific recommendations, we felt confident that the way we were doing things was what worked best for us. We also felt grateful to be able to take our time as we travel. We find it so much more rewarding to immerse ourselves wherever we are. If time is limited, we would recommend selecting fewer sites or countries so that you can stay long enough to see what there is to see, meet some of the people, and fit in time to unwind. There is great value in research and relaxation to optimize traveling experiences.

CHAPTER 3

In Search of a Priest in Bolivia

This story began seven years ago at a marriage encounter in Jacksonville, Florida. We met Father Tom over the weekend and got to know him quite well. He was understanding and considerate of others and always listened carefully before sharing his thoughts on any issue.

He talked about his two families. The first was his deceased mother and father from Maryland as well as his brothers and sisters whom he visited and loved. The second was his Bolivian family and the poor he had worked with for the twenty-five years he had spent in that country. Father Tom had devoted most of that time helping the destitute, particularly unwed mothers. He spoke excellent Spanish and the local indigenous language and thus could communicate effectively with them. We could visualize him listening to their tales of woe.

His last two years had been spent in the eastern part of the United States doing fund raising for the Maryknoll Order of priests, of which he was a member. He despised fund raising, though realized it was an essential ingredient to being a missionary priest.

On that last Sunday evening, we had a long talk with him at the dinner table.

"I'm going back to Bolivia on Tuesday of this week," he exclaimed with relieved joy.

"You sound excited about going," I responded.

"Yes, I am. It's been the longest two years of my life. I just wasn't cut out for this aspect of the priesthood."

"We're glad you're heading home," said Christine.

"What will you be doing in Bolivia upon return?" I asked.

"The same as before. For the next couple of years, I'll work in family services. Bolivia is a very poor country and some of the people are in desperate need of any assistance they can get. If they need medical assistance, I'll try to find free medical service, or if they need work, I'll attempt to find employment for them. Also, simply listening to their problems can sometimes help," he responded.

"Is it discouraging?" Christine asked.

"Not really, I've become used to the poverty and they're my people. After twenty-five years, I know and understand them," he said enthusiastically.

"You said 'for the next couple of years.' What about after that?" I questioned.

"I hope to retire in Bolivia, if the Maryknoll Order allows me to. It's a very nice place and I can continue working part-time with my people."

Of the missionaries Christine and I have met on our travels, Father Tom has clearly been the most dedicated and loving person we have encountered. He was not self-serving in any way.

We parted with hugs and kisses that evening, telling him in a half joking manner, "If we're ever in Bolivia, we'll look you up."

Fast forward seven years. We have changed our lifestyle and are heading to Bolivia. If we had seriously anticipated such a trip, we would have taken Father Tom's address on that last evening. However, we never thought we would go to that nation.

"Should we look for Father Tom?" I asked Christine.

"That would be pretty difficult," she responded, "Bolivia is a big country and we only know his name and that he's a Maryknoll."

"Maybe I could get an eight hundred number for the Maryknoll Order and see if they can assist," I offered.

Before leaving the United States on our ten-month sojourn to Central and South America, I managed to reach the Maryknoll head office. I explained our situation to a helpful woman on the phone.

"Give me twenty-four hours," she responded, "and I'll see what I can do."

The next day, I called her back. She said, "I'm afraid I can't help much, except to say that we have a few priests in La Paz, but most are in Cochabamba."

"Do you think we can just walk into a mission and ask?"

"Yes, be sure to do so. I think Cochabamba will be your best bet," she advised.

Later that year, we found ourselves at Lake Titicaca in Peru with ample time for a month in Bolivia. Thus, we decided to venture in search of Father Tom.

We arrived in La Paz, Bolivia by bus from Puno, Peru. La Paz is a beautiful city of over a million inhabitants, set in a huge canyon. Other cities and towns on the plateau above the city are visibly engulfed in poverty, as was much of La Paz.

While enjoying the area for several days, we located a Maryknoll center listed in the phone book. The priest there was quite pleasant but said he did not know Father Tom and urged us on to Cochabamba.

"That's where most Maryknolls are located," he responded enthusiastically.

"It's a six-hour bus ride," I explained, then asked, "How are the roads?"

"Well, it's not the United States."

We parted company a bit discouraged. I questioned the feasibility of going that long distance without even knowing if Father Tom lived there.

Christine was much more optimistic. "You never know… he may be there. And even if he isn't, we'll at least get to see that part of the country."

According to our map and guide, the city of Cochabamba is in a valley, in the heart of the Andes Mountain chain. A bus ride there was reported to be beautiful, as it traversed the high altiplano and wound its way through the mountains.

And see the country we did. The road to Cochabamba was good by third world standards. It was paved and the scenery was nothing less than astonishing. It was a crystal-clear day and the views of the Andes were magnificent. Our camera got a workout, as we admired the beauty of the majestic white-capped peaks.

Cochabamba lies in a valley, in the midst of these beautiful mountains. Its temperatures are much warmer than La Paz, which was a relief. The lower altitude helps it to maintain a more moderate climate.

The first clue we found regarding Father Tom was from our *Footprints Guidebook*. It had a reference to a Maryknoll factory outlet, where Indian women sold quality, handmade goods. A young woman at the tourist office provided us with a map and directions to the outlet. It was easy enough to locate, as a bus took us part way and then a brief twenty-minute walk took us to the front door.

The façade of the building wasn't much to look at, but the inside was laced with an array of beautiful handmade textile products. Sweaters, socks, hats, wall hangings, and much more were all made of soft alpaca wool. We enjoyed browsing the goods and ended up purchasing two alpaca scarves. While cashing out, we asked the clerk, in our broken Spanish, about Father Tom.

The response was the familiar, "Sorry, I don't know him." However, she was able to give us directions to a Maryknoll Center about two kilometers away.

The walk in the beautiful sunshine was glorious as we took left and right turns along the back streets, following the woman's directions. Short sleeved shirts were the order of the day while sweaters were needed in the evening. It was hard to believe we were in the midst of the Andes.

Finally, we arrived at an enclave of green grass, shade trees, gorgeous flowers, and a *Maryknoll Missions* sign.

We entered, went to the office, then quickly felt disappointment as the receptionist told us that she did not know Father Tom. Then suddenly, she pointed out the window and said, "Run out and ask that priest walking by. He's been here for thirty years and if anybody knows, he does. Hurry, hurry, before he's gone," she insisted.

Out the door we hurried and presented our tale to a very amiable Father Bill. After a few minutes of hesitation he said, "Yes, yes, yes, Father Tom McBride."

"So, you know him?" Christine asked.

"Well, I'm sorry to say I have some very bad news," he said. "We retired priests all eat breakfast together, but one morning, Father Tom was missing. We initially thought nothing of it as he could've been out saying mass for a sick priest or the like. But an hour or so later, one of our priests went to his apartment and found him lying on the floor."

"What happened?" I asked.

"Father Tom suffered a severe stroke at the young age of sixty-five and never fully recovered." Father Bill then added that the Maryknoll Order had sent him back to the States for recovery, but his condition deteriorated and he passed away.

Father Bill was very kind to us in saying, "I'm certain he's looking down at you right now, very appreciative that you went so far out of your way to see him."

Upon departure, Christine and I speculated that while the Maryknoll Order certainly had good intentions, the return to the United States might very well have been what ended it for Father Tom. His first love was undoubtedly Bolivia and its people. Leaving his adopted home must have broken his heart and demoralized him dramatically.

We were consoled in that although we had not found Father Tom, we had found Cochabamba. We intended to spend only three days, but ended up with ten days there. It would have been easy to remain even longer with all the beauty surrounding us. We understood how Cochabamba had become Father Tom's *Shangri-La*.

Although we were saddened by his death, the experience of searching for Father Tom and locating his home brought closure to a good experience in our lives. We always think of him when we encounter do-gooders in our travels. Father Tom accepted the poor Bolivians for who they were and found joy in helping them.

CHAPTER 4

The Bird Who Wanted a Cracker

We landed midday in Cairns, Australia, in the midst of low clouds and light rain. Visibility was poor as we could barely see the mountains only a few kilometers away. A brief taxi ride brought us to a backpacker lodge located near the center of the small vacation stronghold. After securing a room at the lodge, we walked to the ocean only to find a very rough sea.

We found a a travel office and asked about boats going out to the Great Barrier Reef.

"Eh, maybe stop by in the morning and check," the lady hesitatingly responded.

"It doesn't sound too promising," I said to Christine. "Let's ask at another agency."

The street was lined with travel offices, restaurants, and gift stores, so within a minute or two we were at another travel establishment. I went in to ask about boats to the Reef again, but received the same hesitant response.

"Let's walk around town and enjoy ourselves," Christine suggested. "We can check in the morning as they encouraged us to do."

Our sole intent while visiting Cairns was to snorkel at the Great Barrier Reef. We had planned to make an immediate reservation on a boat heading out to the reef. After our escapade to the outer barrier, we would bus down the East

Coast of Australia. This city was much too touristy for our liking, so hanging around waiting for improved weather was not an alternative we considered. It was to our advantage to find a boat heading out as soon as possible, so we could move on and see other parts of this land down under.

We browsed around town for the rest of the afternoon and had an early dinner. The six-hour flight from Indonesia had tired us, so we prepared to go back to the lodge for an early night's rest. Returning to the room, we passed another travel office, where we inquired about a boat once more.

The young woman was very amiable. She said, "Let me be honest with you. The sea looks horrible and the weather forecast for the next five days is no better. I don't foresee a snorkel boat going out for at least five days."

"Thank you," I said. "We'll have to think our situation over."

That evening, I read that there was a bus going to Townsville at 9:30 a.m. There was also the option of bussing up to the mountains in the morning to see what we could of Queensland. Having only a thirty-day visa for Australia limited the amount of time we could spend waiting to get out to the Reef, as we had a lot more of the country that we wanted to visit. Sydney, Melbourne, the Great Ocean Road, and the Red Center were all on our must-see list, so we were unsure what our next step should be.

We rested well that evening, and after breakfast, we decided to head out to enjoy the mountains. Walking towards the bus, we looked up at the nearby hills, only to find a low cloud cover and mist obscuring any views. There was no doubt in either of our minds that the mountains were not a good option.

Looking at each other, we simultaneously said, "Townsville."

"Can we get to the bus station in time?" Christine asked.

I looked at my watch. "We have twenty-five minutes. Let's give it a try."

Without further hesitation, we hurried back to the backpacker lodge, packed, checked out, and ran to the bus station. Arriving at the station with five minutes to spare, we purchased tickets and were soon heading south. By mid-afternoon, we were in Townsville enjoying the warm sunshine. The ride was our first glimpse at how sparse the Australian population is. Although we passed through a few beach communities, by and large, the trip was devoid of habitation. The green vegetation along the coast was beautiful and different from the dry inland areas we would encounter later on our voyage.

"What a difference a few hundred miles can make," remarked Christine, as our bus drove into Townsville.

While busing south, my lovely wife had read about a backpacker lodge called *Forest Haven*, located on nearby Magnetic Island. Upon arrival at the bus station, we called the facility and received a friendly, "Come on over! We have plenty of space. Just catch the four o'clock ferry."

Thus began one of the most memorable ten days of our travels. Friendly people, wonderful weather, a gorgeous island, and an abundance of birds and animals all made for a wonderful adventure. To top all of that off, a boat stopped by the island every morning on its way to the Great Barrier Reef.

Visiting in the off-season allowed the lodge to allocate a kitchen area and several bedrooms to the two of us. "Don't worry," the woman said to us, "You'll have it to yourself for as long as you stay."

Speaking with the owner of the lodge that evening, I mentioned how it sounded like there were a lot of birds around.

"Come out in the morning at seven-forty-five and have a look for yourself. That's when I feed them," he suggested.

The next morning, the man came out with a platter of cooked oatmeal. Approximately seventy-five colorful lorikeets came down from the trees for breakfast. As I sat at a picnic table watching, some landed on my arms, head, and shoulders, as well as on the table. Christine loved taking the photos and we both enjoyed the birds immensely.

Later, we caught the island's shuttle bus to one of the many isolated coves for a day of sunbathing, swimming, and snorkeling. The hilly island is dotted with a series of rocky coves and beaches, while the interior had many trails for hiking and observing the flora and fauna of the island.

That evening, we grilled our emu steak in the company of an English chef. He had been head chef at a restaurant for twelve years, but was offered the opportunity to take a year off to travel, with his job being held until he returned.

Over the years, we have learned that Europeans, particularly British and Germans, have it right when it comes to vacations. Although a year is exceptional, six weeks off per year seems to be the standard, which far exceeds anything Christine or I had ever been accustomed to in the United States.

Mentioning the lorikeets to Geoff the chef, he responded, "Wait a few minutes and we'll be visited by some possums. Here—take a banana to feed them."

Sure enough, within five minutes, two of the furry creatures appeared, looking for dinner. Unlike North American possums, they were friendly and covered with black and white fur, and they sort of hopped along. The cuddly little things were much different from the stringy-tailed possums we were used to seeing. The little creatures kept us company for the remainder of the evening and joined us on subsequent occasions.

After dinner, we went for a stroll around town, only to encounter rock wallabies coming out of the woods. Although they seemed a bit timid, Christine managed some photos, even in the dark. These distant relatives of kangaroos are nocturnal, so we often saw them on our nightly strolls. The island seemed to have a host of natural wonders waiting for us at every turn. It was one of those times when you simply enjoy just being there.

The next day, we caught a boat to the Great Barrier Reef. Kelsey Reef, about a two-hour boat ride from Magnetic Island, is one of those portions of the Great Reef adorned with an abundance of beautiful coral. Although we had the options of fishing, viewing from a glass bottomed boat, or snorkeling, we chose the latter for the entire day. The calm sea was perfect for snorkeling. The day trip included a complete buffet lunch, which broke up the day nicely. It was another gorgeous sunny day which made the fish and coral all the more vibrant with shades of pinks, greens, and blues. Although we have seen more beautiful and colorful fish while snorkeling other reefs, the coral on the Great Barrier Reef was by far the most stunning and even better than we had anticipated.

A brief film and lecture on our journey out helped us to understand the workings of the reef and its coral. The need to protect this natural marvel of nature was emphasized. Reefs are destroyed by commercial fishermen and sportsmen. The former dynamite them to kill the fish for easy picking, while the latter destroy by walking on and picking at these wonders. Simply touching the coral is destructive.

Hiking the hills of Magnetic Island, we spotted slow-moving koala bears munching on eucalyptus trees. One mama koala had a baby's arm protruding from her pouch. We found it exciting to observe these species in their native habitat.

While on a similar hike one day, we stopped on a cliff overlooking the village below with the ocean in the distance. The view was simply magnificent. "Look at that noisy flock of cockateels," I said, while pointing in the direction of some ten to fifteen of the beautiful white birds flying below.

"Yes, noisy but beautiful," Christine stated as the birds flew our way. To our amazement, they came right towards us and landed on a pine tree less than ten feet from our observation point. It was stunning. Why they flew to that particular tree at that moment was beyond our comprehension, but we certainly took pleasure in the moment.

Our conversations continued to dwell on the number of encounters with nature we were experiencing, as well as the domesticity of these wild animals. Their relationship to man seemed much more relaxed and forthcoming than we had ever experienced previously. (Several years later, we visited the Galapagos Islands and once again encountered many friendly creatures.)

The next day, we decided to take a shuttle bus as far north on the island as possible, then hike to a distant beach. Because of its isolation, we were the only people on this sandy cove surrounded by a lush pine forest. We began the day with some swimming and snorkeling, followed by reading on the sunlit beach. It was our last day of relaxation before venturing on a twenty-eight-hour bus ride to Alice Springs in the center of the country, so we were committed to just lazing around.

Always prepared, Christine had brought along some crackers for snacking throughout the day. Being in such an isolated area, there were no vendors within fifteen kilometers, so the crackers were our only means of sustenance.

While looking at Christine, who was at my side and eating a cracker, I noticed something flicker to my immediate front. Turning my head, I was amazed to see a robin-sized black and white bird, strutting about between my legs.

"Look," I said, pointing to the striking intruder.

"I think he wants a cracker," Christine intoned in a low voice, so as not to scare him off.

"You must be right." I held a piece of cracker between my legs and sure enough, he snacked right out of my hand. Needless to say, in the throes of our enjoyment, we gave as much to the bird as we ate ourselves. He was our guest for the remainder of the afternoon. Although a little hungry at the end of the day, we would not have exchanged our experience for a steak dinner.

We ended up spending ten days on Magnetic Island and could have easily remained a month, had it not been for our desire to see other parts of this vast nation. Never before had we seen this many wild animals over such a brief period of time. The friendliness of all these amazing creatures enhanced the experience. With photographs aplenty and many fond memories, we left the island with a bit of sadness in our hearts. We would miss this beautiful part of Australia.

CHAPTER 5

Eight Years in Mexico Without a Visa

Seven years ago, when we departed from our apartment in Charleston, South Carolina, we vowed to look for a place to retire as we traveled the world. We would be looking for a warm climate, access to nearby beaches, a reasonable cost of living, pleasant people, and enough cultural activities to keep us entertained. We knew that someday our travel legs would wear down and we would have to settle.

Oaxaca, a city in southern Mexico, was one of the first places we considered. Having spent a week there two years back, we decided to have a closer look.

Upon arrival, we quickly found a furnished apartment and settled in for a two-month stay. It would be a welcomed break from our on-the-go schedule.

A furnished apartment gave Christine the opportunity to partake in one of her favorite pastimes, cooking. Needless to say, I benefit also. Home cooked meals are a relief from the monotony of constantly eating out. Eating at restaurants all the time may sound like a luxury, but as neither of us are particularly fond of fast food, looking for both good and inexpensive eateries can be a daunting task.

We consider the climate in Oaxaca to be perfect. Most of the year, it reaches eighty-five to ninety degrees Fahrenheit by mid-day, with very little humidity. This is accompanied by lots of brilliant sunshine with only a few cumulus clouds. There are two seasons: dry and rainy. During the dry season, there is no rain, and in the midst of the rainy season, there are occasional late afternoon showers. In fact, it is a stretch, in my opinion, to call it a rainy season. Much of Mexico is semi-arid and Oaxaca is a prime example. Unfortunately for the Mexican farmer, the nation gets too little rain.

Along with good weather, the people of this area are very pleasant. There is a much stronger indigenous influence in the southern part of the country, as opposed to central or northern Mexico, and we find this most amicable. Northern Mexico has a strong influence from the States accompanied with the historical Spanish impact. The far south has a strong contingent of indigenous people who maintain many of their traditional ways. We often refer to San Miguel Allende as Little America, with as many gringos in the town as Mexicans.

Oaxaca's architecture has a pronounced Spanish influence. Founded about five hundred years ago by the Spaniards, it reflects the Iberian Peninsula's style of building with its many Catholic churches and porticos. The *zocalo* public square or park is a main feature to most of Mexico's cities and towns, with this city being no exception. The shaded park is surrounded by buildings with porticos containing restaurants and small cafes. The colorful inhabitants and vendors add much ambiance to the park. I can sit there for hours, simply watching the locals stroll along. It is heart-warming to see young mothers and fathers with their children entranced in the wonder of play. I sometimes sit and have my shoes shined just to immerse myself in the place, not because my footwear is in need of enhancement.

The city also has a symphony orchestra which features classical music. On one memorable evening, we were walking back to our apartment when we heard music coming from the beautiful Santo Domingo church. Upon entering, we found the symphony playing a rendition of Mozart. The combination of the music and setting was divine. The church was completely rehabilitated in the 1970s with gold leaf and is rather glamorous. The rosary chapel to the side is also quite elegant. I often stopped in for five minutes to admire the ornate church while walking to and from our flat. Even the walk to our apartment was a joy, as the cobblestone street was off limits to motor vehicle traffic and lined with buildings of antiquity.

Monte Alban is a mountain adjacent to the city whose top was flattened centuries ago by the Zapotec Indians. It is presently a massive archeological site. National museums like this are free in Mexico on Sundays so locals with limited income can visit and get an understanding of their nation's history.

Christine and I savored the opportunity of renewing our marriage vows in the midst of these ruins, overlooking the greater Oaxaca valley. With birds and wild flowers in abundance, it was a beautiful setting to affirm our marriage. Mexico has a number of archeological sites and this city is fortunate to have this remnant nearby.

Every day of the week, including weekends, one of the adjacent Indian towns has its market day. We have been to all of the markets at one time or another and recommend going to at least one in effort to get a feel for the indigenous towns. Chickens, flowers, goats, vegetables, clothing, and many other goods are all haggled over, as the art of bargaining is at its best. Enjoying a tortilla cooked over charcoal with Oaxaca cheese, epazote herb, and squash flowers is my favorite treat on such occasions. The indigenous flavor of these towns is still evident in spite of the occasional tourists and we always enjoy visiting them.

Walking away from the Zaachila market one fine day, we saw a restaurant advertising goat on its sign.

"Let's give it a try," Christine suggested.

I was agreeable, never having had goat before and always willing to try a local delicacy. Indeed, it was delicious, served with rice and vegetables in a not-too-spicy sauce. However, across the field from the open-air restaurant was a pasture with a herd of goats. Had we observed them earlier, we might have been hesitant to indulge in the meal. Eating a meal is one thing, seeing it on the hoof while you eat is another.

We always enjoy meeting expatriates in a place like Oaxaca. Through the library, public functions, and our apartment complex, we have met several people who have retired or temporarily made their home there. Jim, Bob, and I were neighbors. We would sit outside in our shaded garden, talking for hours, reveling in our various tales.

I vividly remember a conversation with Jim, who had lived in Oaxaca for ten years. I had asked him what type of Mexican visa he had.

"Well, it's like this, Richard. You really don't need a visa if you do it right."

"I thought you needed an FM2 or an FM3."

"Let me tell you how it is." He went on, "My children live in San Diego, which is right over the border, so there's nothing to it."

Don't tell me this seventy-eight-year-old hires a coyote to smuggle him over the border, I thought to myself. I had to question further as my curiosity grew. You hear many stories in Mexico about illegal border crossings, but they usually involve Mexicans not U.S. citizens.

"Do you hire a coyote?"

"Nothing that difficult at all," he responded. "I fly from Oaxaca to Mexico City and change from one gate to another without leaving the domestic terminal. I then fly to Tijuana and take a taxi from the airport to the border."

"What then?" I asked with much intrigue.

He continued, "I simply cross the border with a small bag in one hand and my driver's license in the other. If immigration officials ask how long I've been in Mexico, I simply tell them I stayed the night to do some shopping. My children then pick me up on the United States' side of the border."

"What about the return trip?"

"It's the same. I tell Mexican immigration that I'm staying the night for some shopping and show them my driver's license. After that, the domestic flights present no problem," he concluded.

"Have you been doing that for ten years?" I inquired.

"No, just eight years. Before that, I went through the gyrations and expense of an FM3. Then I wised up."

Jim was a financial analyst who had learned more than finance, I thought to myself. I just could not fathom living in a country without a visa, simply because I did not like to go through their paperwork. I must confess that his scheme was rather simple and worked well enough, as it had been over eight years and he had never been caught. Was it worth it, I wondered? Christine and I concluded not, at least for ourselves.

33

Jim has since passed away, but I often wonder how long he would have been able to get away with sneaking over the border with the changes September 11, 2001 brought.

Although Mexico suffers through bouts of inflation and currency deflation, Oaxaca remains a place of beauty and is inhabited by wonderful people. We have returned on several occasions, usually staying for a month or two, always rejoicing in the city, its people, and its environs. We keep in touch with people in that city via email, and will surely return again. It continues to remain on our list of probable retirement sites.

CHAPTER 6

Buying an Emerald in Phnom Penh

Having arrived in Siem Reap, Cambodia by boat in mid-afternoon, we were eager for our first glance of Angkor Wat and its surrounding temples. We soon found a guesthouse, then employed a motorcycle driver as our driver-guide for the next four days. Although he spoke minimal English, he effectively communicated his desire to drive us to a hill to watch the sunset. We agreed, and after a quick late lunch, we were on our way. Three on a motorcycle is not unusual in most of the world, and thus we set off from town.

Over the past four years, we had continually heard tales from fellow travelers of the grandest of all archeological sites in Asia. "Angkor Wat is the biggest . . . Symmetrical and beautiful . . . You cannot begin to see it in one day . . . Don't leave out Ta Prohm" were just a few of the many comments we heard regarding Angkor Wat.

Christine and I are very interested in archeological sites. We had read a lot about Angkor Wat and were cherishing the opportunity to see the place firsthand. Archeological sites like Angkor always have us wondering at the grandness of these former kingdoms. How much knowledge did they have and how much has been lost? All that we see today are the remains of the things made of stone and cement with some bone fragments and odd ceramics. Remnants of cloth and parchment tend to be lost, as is their knowledge of science, philosophy, or mathematics. Any society creating the likes of Angkor Wat or Machu Picchu must have had substantial knowledge beyond architecture and stone masonry.

Though we enjoy visiting these sites, we also question the impact of tourists on the local culture. Though the financial impact may be positive, how much authenticity remains when the visitors have left? Locals will often compromise their entire lifestyle to gain a dollar, while the traditional agricultural ways are set aside. Much of their religion and culture are lost, as the young focus on serving the needs of the tourism industry.

To our surprise, the hill our driver took us to was Phnom Bakheng. It featured views of the sunset in the west and the temple of Angkor Wat in the east. With binoculars in hand, we were awe-struck as we got a sense of the entirety of the park from our vantage point. We were filled with joy and anticipation for the next day, when we would be hiking and climbing in and about its many nooks and crannies.

The sunset was beautiful, though dominated by thunderous clouds rapidly advancing in our direction. We watched as long as we could, then ran down the hill to avoid the rain. Unfortunately, we did not reach the little thatch hut in time and the rain poured down upon us. The amount of rain over the next half hour was extraordinary. It came down in sheets that stood out against the dark green jungle. An hour later, our driver returned us to town. Arriving at the guesthouse drenched, we dried off and settled in for a good night's sleep.

The next morning, we got an early start and spent most of the day at Angkor Wat. I should explain that there is a large temple which is Angkor Wat. This temple is then surrounded by a multitude of other temples, which cover thousands of acres. This entire area is also often referred to, by travelers, as Angkor Wat. Each individual temple within this massive area has its own name and is worthy of explorations.

The massive temple grounds of Angkor Wat temple and its moat were built around the 12th century, during the rule of the Khmer Empire, which included what is now Cambodia and portions of current Thailand. The immensity and scale of the temple is impressive. At the gateway, the magnificence of the temple strikes you with its typical Khmer conical towers.

We were able to visit the Terrace of Honor, the Gallery of Bas Reliefs, and the Gallery of One Thousand Buddhas as the day wore on. However, most enthralling was the climb around the main tower which dominates the complex. With our adventurous spirit and no boundary ropes, we had the freedom to explore. We speculated that within a couple of years, the government would likely limit the activities of tourists in effort to protect the site. More and more travelers visit Angkor each year, with very few restrictions at present. In order to protect these remains, some preventive measures will need to be taken.

Because of the heat and humidity, we were exhausted by 3 p.m. We retired to our relatively cool room, decidedly happy that we had started out bright and early, before the full strength of the sun could be felt.

The next morning, we toured Angkor Thom with its Terrace of Carved Elephants and Carvings of the Leper Kings. This was a comfortable area to tour as it is set amongst a group of shade trees. Later in the day, we visited the spectacular Temple of Bayon, which has large carved faces adorning some fifty towers. Though the carving detail is not as impressive as other sites, the total composition of the temple was inspiring.

The next day, I visited a myriad of small temples as Christine rested. On the fourth day, we went to my favorite, Ta Prohm. Although it is small in comparison and only took us two hours to explore, it has a memorable, magical ambiance about it. Instead of being completely cleared and restored, it remains ragged with the omnipresence of the jungle enveloping large portions of it. The feature movie *Tomb Raider* depicts Ta Prohm very well, as many scenes were shot here.

After a twenty-kilometer ride through the countryside, we spent the remainder of the day getting a second look at Angkor Wat. It was our last look, and it was very scintillating.

The following day, we caught a four-hour boat ride through Tonle Sap, the large lake that dominates the Cambodian landscape, then went on to the capital, Phnom Penh. We had limited expectations for the city as we had not heard great things. Large, crowded, polluted, and difficult to get around were just a few of the words used to describe this metropolitan area. Although these descriptions are by and large accurate, we were still able to find plenty of charm.

It has become increasingly difficult to find beauty in the large cities of the twenty-first century. The massive influx of people and increasing automotive traffic creates intolerable pollution. With inadequate sewerage systems and little to no trash collection, these metropolitan areas are in desperate need of attention.

On the very day of our arrival in Phnom Penh, a brand-new shuttle bus service was introduced to comfortably transport people around the inner city. We speculated that it was probably the first air-conditioned public bus in the country. It enabled us to breathe easier as we moved throughout the city.

Over the next few days, much of our time would be spent looking for the perfect emerald. Some years back, Christine had acquired a ring which was in need of a stone. We had waited until Phnom Penh because we had read and were told that good quality sapphires and emeralds would be available at reasonable prices. The challenge was to find a stone that she really liked and that would fit the setting. While taking in the sites of the city, we found ourselves walking into every jewelry and precious stone establishment we could find. The stones just never seemed to have the right clarity or simply did not fit the dainty setting.

"Sorry, we'll keep on looking," became our all too familiar expression.

A bone-jarring, fifteen-kilometer ride on the rear of a motorbike took us to the Killing Fields. Approximately one hundred fifty mass graves containing thousands of victims made this a very chilling experience. Skulls of many bodies that had been exhumed were on display. It was a grim reminder of the many atrocities that continue to take place in what we consider a civilized world. It is estimated that as many as one quarter of Cambodia's population lost their lives during Pol Pot's rule.

A much more pleasant experience was our visit to the Foreign Correspondents Club, overlooking the Tonle Sap River. Though the menu was limited, the historical ambience of the place was marvelous. It provides the most authentic sense of the 1920s that I have ever experienced. The riverside colonial atmosphere with its balcony overlooking the flowing water is pure nostalgia for an era long gone by.

College students were putting on a traditional dance and song recital, which was interesting and entertaining from a cultural perspective. It demonstrated the energy going into the nation's recovery. These people that had been put down so horribly were fighting back and rebuilding their society and nation with whatever means available. With time and support, they will have created something to be proud of.

Visiting a foreign land and not going to the market is unimaginable to Christine. In addition to the variety of foods and goods, one also gets a sense of the inhabitants and their culture while strolling through these beehives of activity. Phnom Penh's Central Market was no disappointment, as we wandered amongst the various stalls with droves of people negotiating their deals. After an hour or so, we came across a series of gemstone establishments which piqued our interest.

"Let's try one of these stores," Christine suggested. I enthusiastically followed.

The salesman must have had a thousand, if not more, emeralds and sapphires, all under glass and distributed in small trays. A girl who appeared to be his twelve-year-old daughter, stood beside him, ready to provide us with assistance. The young girl spoke a little English while her father spoke not a word of the language.

Christine showed the ring with the empty setting to the two enterprising attendants. They looked at each other, smiled, and pointed in the direction of one of the display cases. It took close to thirty minutes to select the perfect gem to fit the ring. The stone Christine selected was a beautifully clear, dark emerald.

"How much?" Christine asked.

"Four thousand," the little girl answered.

I looked at Christine and questioned," Did she mean four thousand riels?"

"I think so, let me ask again."

"Four thousand riels?" Christine asked the girl. The girl nodded yes.

"That's about one dollar," I told Christine. The Cambodian riel was about 3800 to the dollar at the time. "This doesn't make sense," I remarked.

"Let's buy the stone," said Christine.

"We need to have it set," I said, while pointing to the ring. The little girl understood our problem, and told us she knew a stone setter who could help.

"Pay and follow me," she instructed.

It is normal to negotiate in Cambodia, but for one dollar, we set the formality aside and gave the man his four thousand riels, then followed his daughter in hopes of having the stone set.

Always smiling, the girl led us through the market taking left and right turns through alleys lined with vendors. Following her for about fifteen minutes provided us with an extensive tour of the massive Central Market and a good sense of its diversity.

Finally, we turned a right corner and stopped at an elderly gentleman sitting behind a two-foot-wide table. He had a magnifier over his right eye and was working on a bracelet. Our young escort began speaking rapidly in Cambodian to the man and then directed us to hand over the ring and stone.

Christine did so without question. Normally, we would ask how much but we were so entranced by the entire experience that we just stood in awe.

In less than five minutes, the man returned the ring with the stone firmly set in place. After a careful examination, Christine looked at the man and asked, "How much?"

The man and girl entered into an extensive discussion, then the girl looked at us and said, "Four thousand."

I stood there staring in amazement as Christine counted the money.

"Let's give the girl something," I said to Christine. But before I could get my hand in my pocket, the girl waved goodbye and dashed off.

"Thank you!" we exclaimed as she hurried away.

Christine looked at me and asked, "Do you think it's real?" pointing to the ring.

"I doubt it, but who knows?"

The stone was beautiful, and after several years of use, it is as nice as ever and still firmly set in place. As for the eight thousand riels or two dollars, we would have paid more than that just for the experience. Watching that young girl march us through the market with that smile on her face will always be imbedded in our minds. The pleasures of observing people at work can be very rewarding.

The process of buying that emerald was one of the true joys of traveling in Cambodia, exemplifying how simple things in life can be so overwhelmingly fulfilling.

CHAPTER 7

Two Nights in Dhaka

The travel agent in Kathmandu spoke excellent English and with an in-depth explanation, told us that staying one night in Dhaka would not be a problem. Biman Bangladesh, the national airline, would put us up for the night and we would fly on to Burma (Myanmar) at 10:25 the next morning. It was the best way to fly from Nepal to Burma, and by far the least expensive.

Although we had no interest in being in Dhaka, it seemed easy enough and the price of the flights was right at $139 each. We happily accepted our tickets, set aside the explanation, and went about our explorations of Nepal for the next two weeks.

A couple of weeks later, as we handed over our tickets to the airline attendant at the Biman Bangladesh desk, she looked at us with seat assignments and said, "Two nights in Dhaka."

"No, no," Christine immediately responded.

"Sorry," she said in her broken English, "Biman pay for one night."

Christine and I looked at each other with disappointment. "Two nights in Dhaka it is."

The flight took off on schedule without a hitch and upon arrival at Dhaka Airport, we picked up our luggage and went directly to immigration. With a smile on his face, the official looked at us and said, "One hundred twenty U.S. dollars each for a visa."

"One hundred twenty each?" I repeated, then explained how we were only staying two nights, and not by choice.

The only response we could get from the man was, "One hundred twenty U.S. dollars each for a visa."

It felt like a broken record. Finally, I asked, "Is there a transit lounge?"

He responded by pointing in the direction of the transit area.

Setting down our luggage and taking a seat on the bench, we resigned ourselves to spending two nights in the lounge. We had no interest in Bangladesh and certainly had not budgeted $240 for visas. Although we had time on our hands, we did not have that kind of spare cash.

After a half hour, I said, "I'm going over to that Biman Bangladesh office," pointing to a corner desk.

"Give it a try," Christine suggested. "I doubt if they can do anything about immigration though."

I admonished myself to keep my cool, although I was boiling inside.

The official looked at me while I approached and asked, "Can I help you?"

"Yes, we just flew in from Nepal and are flying to Myanmar in two days and were wondering if you might be of assistance," I said, as I prepared to further plead our case.

Before I could continue, he interjected, "Don't worry. I will take care of everything." Not giving me a chance to speak, he went on, "You get your luggage while I arrange for your limo, hotel, and food."

"What about immigration?" I quickly asked.

"Don't worry about anything," he answered.

Without further ado, I returned to Christine, feeling like a knight in shining armor. After a brief explanation, we returned to the airline desk and the attendant said, "You give me your passports and I will give you these chits which will serve as your visas for two days."

We looked at each other with hesitation. One of the rules of travel is to never, ever give up your passport to anybody.

Christine daringly exclaimed, "What else can we do? Sit here for forty-eight hours?"

"Nothing to worry about," he stated, "just give me your passports and I'll have them for you when you return."

After we handed over our passports, he said, "Come, follow me." He carried Christine's pack and led us on our way. The funniest thing about our brief walk to the limo was walking right by the immigration official who had attempted to get us to pay the $120 each. I walked by him with a big grin on my face. He did not ask for our passports or the cardboard chits, which were stamped with the numbers thirty-one and thirty-two. In fact, nobody asked for our visas over the next two days, which may have been a good thing; neither of us believed a cardboard chit with nothing but a number stamped on it really served as a visa.

The airline employee not only escorted us to the limo, he also accompanied us to a very nice airport hotel. Leaving nothing to chance, he explained to the hotel clerk that the airline would be responsible for our expenses.

He then turned to us stating, "The limo will pick you up at eight-thirty the morning after next. Enjoy your two nights in Dhaka."

Enjoy Dhaka we did.

We dined on excellent meals from the hotel restaurant, served in our air-conditioned room. Having left England more than three months back, we had not experienced this sort of luxury since then.

Neither of us had ever anticipated visiting Bangladesh, so we lacked information about the country. We had no maps or guidebooks for assistance. We hadn't even ever met a traveler who had been there.

Fortunately, the desk clerk was a bundle of information regarding buses, ferries, and general knowledge about Dhaka, though he did not have a map. He suggested that we attend the celebrations in the park, walk through the market, and take a ferry ride up the river and back.

Without hesitation, we set out to accomplish as much as possible in our one-day stay. Although the place was completely foreign to us, the people we had met thus far had been very friendly.

The bus stop was immediately in front of our hotel. The next morning, after enjoying a hearty breakfast, we made our way to the center of the capital city for a mere ten cents.

It just so happened that it was the New Year's celebration in Bangladesh that day and the city was bursting with festivities. We made our way to the park and partook of local foods, drink, and merriment. Thousands of people were being entertained with music while picnicking on the grass. Children played in the midst of it all.

The only peculiarity was that we were cordoned off from walking through a small area around one of the monuments. It was a minor issue and we easily walked around the obstacle.

After several hours in the park, we took a bike rickshaw to the river area. The hotel clerk had explained to us that it would be nice if we took a ferry upriver and then catch another for the return voyage. It would be a pleasant means of seeing the countryside, he suggested.

Arriving at the dock, a friendly ticket salesperson explained how we could catch a ferry leaving in a few minutes, travel about forty kilometers upstream, but then we would have to catch a bus back to the city.

The rivers are the main avenues of transportation in Bangladesh as the nation is a massive low-lying delta. Although a convenient form of getting around, the rivers also serve up much sorrow in the form of floods during heavy monsoons and typhoons. Thousands of lives have been lost over the years during typhoon season, as uncontrollable waters inundate the low area. However, this day was beautiful with ample sunshine and a pleasant breeze. What really made the day for us were the friendly people we met while boating upstream. They served up an entertaining commentary of the various things we cruised by.

Most helpful was a forty-one-year-old man, named John. He boarded the ferry at the ten-kilometer mark and introduced himself in impeccable English. He felt we might need assistance, as we were the only two westerners he had seen on a ferry in months and we looked out of place. He was probably eager to practice his second language. Whatever his motives were, we were delighted to have his company.

John had served twenty years in the National Army as a volleyball player. His athletic prowess had enabled him to see much of the world, which also prompted him to learn English.

Over the next two hours, our escort informed us about the ins and outs of the nation's people, geography, and its army. He treated us like royalty and we were very appreciative.

When we were approaching our exit port, he explained that it would be quite difficult for us to locate the bus returning to Dhaka, so he exited with us and walked us to the transport. He explained to the conductor precisely where we were to be let off in the capital. All of this was accomplished with the graciousness of a born diplomat.

What made us all the more appreciative was knowing that he would have to return to the dock and catch the next ferry going north. It would have been much simpler for him to have remained on the original ferry and wave us off. He had gone way out of his way for us and we let him know how grateful we were for his hospitality and that of his nation.

With no difficulty, we found our way back to Dhaka and then to the hotel, where we were treated to a delicious Chinese dinner.

The only unsettling matter to our entire Dhaka experience was that we learned from the next day's newspaper that several people had been seriously hurt when a bomb exploded in the park during the New Year's merriment. We wondered if the bomb had detonated in the cordoned off area of the park that we had to avoid the previous day.

The next morning, the limousine picked us up at the appointed time, and the same Biman Bangladesh official that had escorted us to the hotel, greeted us for our return to the airport. With our passports in hand, he directed us to the airplane and bid us farewell, asking, "Hope you enjoyed your two nights in Dhaka?"

Indeed, our two nights in Dhaka had turned out to be very special—wonderful interactions with kind and friendly people in a lovely land.

CHAPTER 8

Phosphorescence at Three in the Morning

One of the more delightful places we have been is the island of Bali in Indonesia. It has a tropical climate with pleasant people and is very scenic.

On our first trip to that little paradise, we were looking for a peaceful location by the ocean to lay back. The past few months had us constantly on the move, making our way through much of Southeast Asia. After Indonesia, our plans included two months touring Australia and then New Zealand. Sandwiched in between, we had a sixty-day Indonesian visa. This gave us enough time to explore a couple of the islands and still indulge in some relaxation.

Friends directed us to an area called Lovina, located on the northern part of the island, stating it was both inexpensive and relaxing. We flew into Denpasar, on the southern end of the island at ten in the evening, and located temporary lodging. The next morning, we took a *bemo* (small Indonesian minivan used as a bus) north. Our hotel in Lovina was comfortable and even had a pool. However, we found it to be a mixed bag. The pool was crowded with tourists and there were vacationers at every turn. In addition, it was impossible to leave the lodging without being confronted by touts trying to sell trinkets, tours, or lunch. At this stage in our travels, we were accustomed to people selling their wares aggressively, but this was overwhelming.

"Let me check out the place Sarah suggested. I think I made a note of it in my diary," Christine suggested.

"Yes, I remember her saying it was east of Singaraja," I responded.

"Here it is, a town called Yeh Sanih. Maybe it's written up in *Lonely Planet*."

We did find it in the guidebook, but little information was available. The next day, we caught a *bemo* for the twenty-kilometer ride. Accommodations were very limited, but we we did locate a small set of bungalows right by the ocean. In fact, the rippling sea was only fifteen meters in front of our deck and the property was lined with coconut trees. While the place had ten cabins, at times we found that we were the sole occupants. Other times, there would be one or two neighboring couples. There were not enough guests for the enthusiastic touts to bother with here. For a mere thirty thousand rupiah, then worth about three to four dollars per evening, we had a comfortable, though not luxurious abode. The price included breakfast, which we enjoyed on our small patio overlooking the Bali Sea. The setting was picture perfect. The beaches on the northern shore of the island were black volcanic sand, and the swimming was ideal with a calm sea.

We relaxed in this setting for three weeks during this first adventure in Indonesia. However, Yeh Sanih has become a standard for us when in search of the easy life.

Fortunately, we came equipped with our hammocks and a good selection of books to read. The hammocks were easily strung up on the veranda, which made the reading very comfortable. In addition to the books, I had my oils for painting and a wholesome array of Balinese birds as my subjects.

In our quest for a retirement spot, we have often considered northern Bali. It has an ideal climate nearly year-round, is commensurate with our budget, and its inhabitants are most amiable. Unfortunately, its sixty-day visa, now thirty-day, is difficult to work around. Many of the retirees living there will fly to Singapore every two months to renew their visas. This is not only inconvenient but also adds tremendously to the expense. We also thought that in the course of time, we would likely become bored. Singaraja is a very nice little capital city, but lacks the host of cultural activities we would desire if making this a permanent retirement residence. We have never completely dismissed it from our list, as its peace and quiet always seems to linger at the back of our cerebral complex.

Nyepi, the Balinese New Year, was being celebrated that first time we were staying in Yeh Sanih. Our host family, who managed the bungalows where we were making our abode, invited us to join them in the festivities. To begin with, they adorned us in Balinese attire. I ended up with a *pareo* around my waist, a white jacket fully buttoned to my neck, which added a touch of formality, and a turban-style white hat. Christine looked luxurious in her sarong, dark lace blouse, and Balinese headgear.

I should explain that the majority of Balinese people are Hindu, although surrounded by Muslims on its neighboring islands. It seems they migrated here from India centuries ago. With its isolation, Bali developed its own set of Hindu traditions, somewhat different from those of India.

On this particular New Year's Eve, we marched down the street to the local temple, dressed in our borrowed garb. The

Balinese women were stunning in their ceremonial dress. In addition to wearing formal attire for the occasion, they balanced a spiral pyramid of fruit which rose fifteen to twenty inches above their heads. Their ability to balance such an extension was both amazing and beautiful to watch.

At the temple, we found offerings in the form of rice and vegetables, laid out approximately four hundred feet from the temple to the sea. The offerings are to lure the demons away from the island, down into the sea. In addition to its religious element, we found it to be a social function with people conversing and playing games. All of it was light spirited and joyous.

New Year's Day is designed to fool the devilish spirits into remaining in the deep ocean and not returning to land. In order to admonish them from coming back, the island is completely quiet for the entire day. The devils are fooled into thinking the place is not inhabited, so they have no desire to visit. I cannot vouch as to whether or not the devils were fooled, but I can lay testimony to the fact that the island was very quiet. There were no vehicles on the road, no televisions playing, and no children at play for the entire day. Families simply sat around the home keeping all noise to a minimum. Our host family had previously agreed to quietly serve us food, although they did not eat. No restaurants or stores were open and the only noise to be heard was the lowly ripple of the ocean. It was an amazing day, truly unique in the annals of our lives.

As I stated before, the calm sea was ideal for relaxing and perfect for swimming. Hence, I found myself in the water four or five times per day and night. Eighty-degree waters are ideal for my liking and so I took advantage of the opportunity presenting itself.

On one particular evening, Christine and I found ourselves so engaged in conversation that we failed to notice the time. Before we knew it, it was 3 a.m.

"I think I'll go in for a quick swim before retiring," I remarked.

"Not a bad idea," Christine agreed.

Within a few minutes, we were a hundred feet out from shore, and to our amazement, we were in the midst of an ocean of phosphorescence. By simply moving our arms or legs, we activated an array of phosphorous, which lit up like a light bulb. It was as if our appendages were magic wands, lit by movement. It was a spectacular sight to behold.

We have returned to Yeh Sanih on a couple of occasions while exploring other portions of Indonesia, always entranced with its peacefulness. It is a wonderful place to kick back. We can only hope that Yeh Sanih will continue to evade the crowds of tourists.

CHAPTER 9

Diving Off a Boat in Ha Long Bay

The combination bus and train ride up the coast of Vietnam was an extraordinary journey. Beautiful beaches and mountains created spectacular views of the countryside and coastline. Although I had been here thirty-five years ago during the war, the immense beauty of the nation was not visible to me then as it was this time. In the intensity of the war, I had failed to see the magnificence of what was before my eyes. Now, with the time and intent, Christine and I were able to appreciate the nation at peace.

Hoi-An is a quaint little city in the central part of the country. It managed to survive the onslaught of both the French and United States wars pretty much unscathed. It was once an important trading port, set beside the Thu Bong River. The architectural remains of its bygone era remain and are very visible as one strolls the alluring streets of town. Japanese, Chinese, and European influences are apparent throughout the city. Its many shops and riverfront restaurants kept us occupied during our leisurely stay. What caught our attention in particular were the many silk shops. Vietnamese silks come in a wide range of colors from subtle to brilliant iridescent shades. It was difficult to select among the broad variety available. With time and patience, we made our choices and a local woman tailor custom-made some quality blouses and shirts for us.

Some of the merchant river houses have now been converted into museums. The old buildings with gorgeous wooden furnishings and artifacts dating back generations were truly beautiful.

A brief journey north had us visiting the ancient imperial city of Hue. The former center of dynasties has escaped the massive industrialization of other Vietnamese cities like Da Nang and Ho Chi Minh City.

Although the ancient citadel lies in ruins, there remains enough intact to appreciate what a glorious past this edifice must have had. The interiors and exteriors imbue the traveler with the ambiance of the former Imperial City. Floating down the Perfume River with its pagodas also gave us a glimpse of this area's ancient glory.

Hanoi was very different than what we had anticipated. We found beauty and elegance in the Vietnamese capital. The heavy industrialization of Saigon was absent, as was the extreme pollution. Although fraught with ample motor vehicle traffic, it somehow has maintained a sense of quaintness. Even the inner city is speckled with lakes and shaded parks which made for engaging walks in the early evening.

The ravages of bombing from thirty years ago were not in any way visible within the city, and in no way did we detect any vengeance towards westerners as a result of past conflicts. We felt welcomed by these very cordial people. They were part of the cosmopolitan world, but also kept their hold on the past. Both the present and history appeared to meet in Hanoi.

The Old Quarter, where we found a comfortable guesthouse, featured architecture from its French Colonial past, while high rise buildings were only a short distance away. Restaurants boasted American, European, and Oriental menus within a wide price range.

Hopefully, Hanoi will continue to languish in its past as the tenacious claws of modernity engulf other cities of this enterprising nation.

The most famous and captivating natural wonder of Vietnam is Ha Long Bay. Four hours from Hanoi, hundreds of limestone outcroppings sit in this enormous bay that straddles the Gulf of Tonkin. The islands have many hidden caves and small bays that add to the intrigue of this mystical area. Many refer to Ha Long Bay as the eighth natural wonder of the world.

We took a voyage in a small, motorized craft for our three-day journey of the bay. Accompanying us were seven former Vietnamese, now naturalized Swedes or Americans. They had been *boat people* as children, and had survived the long treacherous journey through the South China Sea to Singapore, and eventually to their destination country. They told us of their many friends and relatives who were not as fortunate and did not survive the hazardous journey.

All of them had taken on western names. They introduced themselves as John, Sally, Jim and so on. Their company was extremely enjoyable as they welcomed us into the group. We ate, drank, and shared stories over the next few days while plying the waters. Their command of English as well as Vietnamese made for light conversation and enabled them to translate for us while teaching us a bit of the local language.

One afternoon, the captain stopped the vessel and asked if we would like to go in for a swim.

"By all means," exclaimed John. And within minutes, all of our friends were in the water.

Christine and I happily joined them for a great time of frolic.

That evening, we found lodging on the touristy Cat Ba Island and ate at a local Vietnamese restaurant. The real beauty of the island was to be seen at sunrise, as the brilliant red sphere rose over the limestone karst of distant islands. A short walk to a pointed outcropping presented us with views of the archipelago at its best. The array of sharp-needled mountain peaks seemed especially vibrant at sunrise as well as at sunset.

Boating back towards the beachhead on a subsequent afternoon, the captain once again lauded us with the question, "How about a swim?"

Not to be outdone this time, I quickly dashed up the ladder and was the first to reach the rooftop of the boat. On our previous outing, our friends had razzed me for not jumping in the water from the uppermost level. This time, just as the anchor was being dropped, I was the first in from the high perch. However, much to my surprise, the water was very different from our previous excursion. On our last swim, the boat was nestled into the bay of an island which afforded us protection. This time, we were in the throes of an amazingly swift current. Noticing my struggle, Jim threw a life ring towards me. Now I faced the prospect of swimming against the current to reach the boat.

I swam for what felt like an eternity, making very little headway. I could hear Christine, who had wisely delayed entering the water, yelling, "Come on, you can make it!"

Finally, Jim and John dove in after me, assisting me in my return to safety. All ended with laughter and cheering, although I was quite exhausted from the experience.

The captain, for his part, was all apologies. "Sorry, wrong place," he chided himself.

I shook his hand and asked Jim to tell him not to worry, all is well that ends well.

Without further ado, we headed for the safety of an island and we all had an easy, pleasurable swim in the balmy waters of Ha Long Bay.

The bay, the friends, and even the dive off the boat will always be treasured memories of Vietnam.

CHAPTER 10

A Shoeshine at the Golden Temple

Christine insisted we take a week and visit Amritsar, India. Although I had heard of the Sikh religion, I was not familiar with any details, nor did I know its nucleus was the Golden Temple. My wife's upbringing in northern England and her British university experience had broadened her knowledge of India and its religions, way beyond my scope.

We arrived by train from Delhi in the late evening and had difficulty locating a guesthouse. What we eventually found left much to be desired. The abode was small, musty, and dirty, so immediately the next morning, we searched for a more appropriate dwelling place. By late morning, we were settled into a small, clean room, within a large facility on a busy street. Though this city gets many pilgrims visiting the Golden Temple, the complex provides sleeping quarters for most of its followers, hence a limited supply of inexpensive lodging for the odd travelers like us.

The remainder of our first full day was devoted to shopping. India silks are famous throughout the world and with many markets, Amritsar had ample options. For lunch, we enjoyed a *thali* for which the country is so renown. For a mere fifty cents, we had all the rice, vegetables, curry, lentils, and drink one could ever hope for. At first, I was a bit hesitant about using a banana leaf as a plate, but quickly became accustomed and found I quite liked it. Using my hand as an eating implement took a bit more getting used to. The meal was delicious and the amiable servers continued to supply more and more as we emptied our leaves.

The next day, we took a twenty-kilometer motorbike ride to the India-Pakistan border to view the changing of the guard. Several thousand Indian nationals were on hand for the ceremony, though the facility was limited in space. The attendant was most kind in escorting us and two other westerners to front row seats. There were as many, if not more, people on the Pakistan side, partaking in their own formal ceremonious activities.

The entire affair was most impressive with the participants wearing bright uniforms and shining boots. However, what attracted the most attention were the boisterous attendees. The heckling from the other side of the border was just as rambunctious, as the two sides entered a very unceremonious yelling dual. At one point, we were frightened there would be a rush to the gate with an outpouring of violence. Fortunately, the military presence prevailed and the audience gradually dispersed.

With much relief, we retraced our steps to Amritsar and were thankful to reach our hotel in one piece. The animosity between India and Pakistan is very deep seated. One of the areas we most wanted to visit while in this nation was Kashmir, but the perpetual warfare in that part of the country made it impossible.

Early the next morning, we made our way to the infamous park where nearly four hundred Indians were slaughtered at the hands of a British officer and his battalion of troops. The incident happened as the British were attempting to maintain order in the colony in 1919. In addition to the hundreds killed from bullets, over a thousand were wounded or crushed and suffocated as they jumped into a huge well, trying to avoid the gunfire.

Visiting the park was very eerie, as a sense of that moment in history continues to inhabit the atmosphere. The well in which people pinned their hopes is still there, as well as the thousands of bullet holes that dot the brick walls. The park is truly a reminder of man's inhumanity towards his fellow human beings.

Our next venture was the main purpose of our trip to Amritsar. We made our way to the Golden Temple amidst the thousands of pilgrims that visit the religious site every day. One of the great moments in a Sikh's life is when he makes the pilgrimage to the temple. Since our visit, whenever I encounter a Sikh, I mention having visited this beautiful place of worship. The response is always a smile followed by acknowledgement of how fortunate I have been. The Sikhs I have met who have visited this wonder of the world are justly proud of having made the pilgrimage.

Arriving at the temple grounds, we noticed a sign directing visitors to deposit their shoes prior to entering. In an orderly fashion, the attendants handled the mass of footwear, handing each person a claim number with which to collect their shoes upon departure.

We walked through a running pool of water to cleanse our feet before entering. All the floors from this point on were made of marble and were impeccably clean, as was the entire place.

Once through the entrance, we saw the temple resting in the center of a large manmade lake with a marble causeway leading to the main attraction. The dome of the temple is entirely covered with gold leaf, from which it gets its name.

While circumnavigating the lake in the shade of marble columns and uprights, an elderly man approached us and asked us to spend a few moments with him. Following his lead, we sat on the floor facing each other.

Christine and I glanced at each other in delight, cherishing the opportunity to share time with this most amiable person. He wanted to share the major tenets of his religion and impress upon us the importance of the facility surrounding us. We spent nearly half an hour with this mild-mannered man and developed an appreciation for the love, kindness, and peaceful ambience of the Golden Temple and its environs.

The inside of the temple is as breathtaking as its exterior. On this particular Sunday, it was nearly impossible to get inside due to the mass of pilgrims. Weekdays are much less crowded. We were fortunate enough to be able to return on a Tuesday to spend further time inhaling the atmosphere with fewer people about the place. On that Sunday though, we continued our exploration in spite of the crowd. We had heard that thousands of meals were served each day to visitors and that dormitories were provided as sleeping quarters for its faithful and their guests. Although we were not in need of lodging or food, we were interested in seeing it firsthand.

"How in the world could you feed this mass of humanity?" Christine wondered aloud.

"Weekdays, I understand, but it must be challenging on a day like this."

One of the faithful encouraged us to enter the large dining hall and have lunch, so we decided to partake. In an orderly fashion, we followed a crowd into a massive hall where we were directed to sit by a wall beside others. There must have been a thousand or more people in this building, all eager to enjoy the complimentary meal. Within minutes of our being seated, we were presented with trays, followed by a complete vegetarian meal. The entire group was fed in a gracious manner, all in less than half an hour. As we were leaving, I noticed the next throng entering. The organization behind the scenes must have been phenomenal to serve up this amount of food in such a brief period of time.

"Let's have a look at the dormitories," I suggested.

We asked a woman passing by for directions. Within ten minutes, we were at a series of huge dormitories with hundreds, if not thousands, of rooms, all with common baths. The sleeping facilities were packed with occupants preparing for the night's stay. Although crowded by our standards, we were heartened to see everyone sharing in the peace and harmony of the moment.

"It's getting late. We better get a move on," Christine stated.

"Okay, do you think we can return?" I wondered aloud. I could romantically visualize returning on a less crowded day.

"Let's plan on it," she quickly responded.

Upon exiting, we returned to claim our shoes and to my amazement, my shoes had been shined.

"Can you believe the kindness of these people?" Christine noted as she looked at my newly polished footwear.

We later learned that deeds such as shining shoes or preparing food for free distribution were part of the Sikh religion and its commitment to community service. It was a lucky chance that led to my dusty boots being chosen for the shoeshine.

The kindness and generosity of all the pilgrims and volunteers we had encountered that day was truly heart-warming.

CHAPTER 11

The Turtles of San Agustinillo

Christine and I were exhausted and we both felt we needed a good rest. After selling gifts at a series of Christmas shows and then working forty consecutive twelve-hour days at kiosks in malls, the effort began to take its toll. Where would we take our break?

"San Agustinillo will be the perfect place," my darling wife exclaimed as we boarded the bus for the six-hour journey from Oaxaca City to the beaches of southern Mexico.

"I can't wait to lay back in the hammock and listen to the ocean," I romanticized.

We had located the beach by accident two years back while staying in Puerto Angel. While traveling to the village of Mazunte, I mentioned to Christine, "We passed a beach town and the bus didn't even stop. We should go there. It's probably our kind of place."

"It should be quiet and peaceful since the buses don't bother to stop," she enthusiastically added.

The following day, we returned to find the beach to our liking. It was a white sand beach with rolling waves and very few gringos.

That first year, we had only lingered a few days, and the next year, we stayed for a week. On this occasion, we planned to remain for two weeks before embarking on our seven-month exploration of Mexico.

The first few days were exactly as planned. They involved nothing but pure relaxation as we read books while swinging in our hammocks under the shade of a palapa. The roar of the ocean, a light breeze, and a dip in the water every now and then added up to perfection.

On the fourth evening came the news.

There was a loud knock on the door of our room. I looked at Christine. "Who could that be?"

"I don't know. I'll go see," she answered, while heading to the door.

"Hurry! Hurry! Come down to the beach! A turtle is laying her eggs," Peter told us excitedly.

Peter and Rose were a couple staying at the same guesthouse as us. We had met them the previous day and shared many stories while enjoying the beach. They were very pleasant, and having traveled much of Mexico, were able to share much-needed advice for our Mexican adventure.

"We'll be right with you," I said, as I rushed to put on a shirt.

"Where on the beach?" asked Christine.

"Immediately in front of the palapa."

Within minutes, we were on our way to the beach to get in on the excitement. And there she was—a huge turtle that must have weighed one hundred fifty pounds, depositing dozens of eggs in the hole she had dug in the sand. We watched in amazement under the light of a full moon. On completion, she buried the eggs by shoveling sand over them with her flippers. She then quickly made her departure into the ocean, never to see her offspring. Fortunately, our presence had not altered her behavior.

After she left, we marked the exact spot with a stone. Rose then cautioned, "We ought to shuffle the sand in effort to cover the scent, otherwise dogs will smell these and have them dug up by morning."

We took her advice seriously and found branches to serve as rakes. We covered the turtle tracks to and from the sea, as well as the immediate area around the nest. I then went to the room and got some talcum powder to sprinkle around the area, in effort to further disguise any evidence of our maternal friend.

As Rose and Peter returned to their room, Christine suggested we take a walk on the beach. It has been our practice to take moonlit walks on the beach as frequently as possible. It is a quiet and romantic way to end the day.

"Wouldn't it be amazing to stick around and see the babies hatch?" she mentioned as we strolled along.

"It certainly would."

"I wonder how long it takes for turtle eggs to incubate."

"Why don't we go to the turtle museum tomorrow. We'll get as much information as possible," I suggested.

Fortunately, the museum was only five kilometers away, so the next morning, we set out on our quest.

Never having been to this particular place before, we found the experience entertaining as well as informative. Our Mexican guide did not speak English so our little knowledge of Spanish was helpful.

We learned that the female turtle returned to the same beach throughout her life to lay eggs, and nearly always did so between November and March. The incubation period is between forty-three and forty-five days and the eggs would hatch in the early morning, probably around 4 a.m.

We also learned that the museum had been erected several years prior as an economic alternative to the turtle-fishing industry. To our amazement, we were in the midst of what had been a turtle-processing center. The guide told us about an old plant that processed two thousand turtles per day. By closing down the plant, the government had attempted to create other forms of employment by energizing the tourist industry, but unfortunately for the locals, the effort had achieved limited success.

On our walk back from the museum, we stopped by the area of the former plant. All that remained was a foundation overgrown by vegetation, as well as a hilltop water tank.

At the rate of slaughtering two thousand per day, it is not difficult to see why turtles became an endangered species.

Upon arrival at our abode, Christine implored, "Let's stay. Let's wait out the forty-five days and watch them hatch."

"What about the rest of Mexico?"

"We'll still have five months, and besides, when else will we have the opportunity to experience anything like this? It's a once-in-a-lifetime and we can see Mexico anytime."

We decided that morning to see it through and it turned out to be a very rewarding forty-five days.

Remaining at the same beach for an extended period of time can get a bit tiresome, so we had to dig into our bag of tricks to occupy ourselves. To begin with, we decided to dedicate at least one day per week to an entirely different adventure. On one occasion, we bused to San Agustin for some of the finest snorkeling imaginable. The colors and abundance of fish were amazing. Another time, we hiked inland to take in some swimming at the base of a waterfall. Several times, we made our way into Puerto Escondido, a much larger beach town with an assortment of tourist facilities, to which we happily availed ourselves. These trips also provided us the opportunity to restock our book supply and converse with English-speaking people. Many Canadian tourists from British Columbia winter in this city and we found them to be welcomed company.

Back on the beach, we kept an eye on the rock that marked the nesting spot. In addition to reading, we enjoyed bird watching and went on lengthy walks, admiring the many colorful species. I also had a carving knife with me and satisfied my artistic interest by whittling birds out of driftwood.

Although Rose and Peter had moved on, other couples stopped in for a few days at a time and we would share our tale of the turtle that laid her eggs. The days and weeks went by quickly and as the forty-third day approached, Margaret and Antoine, a young couple from Montreal, arrived at the beach. We told them about the turtles and without hesitation, Antoine exclaimed, "I'll share the watch with you."

The plan was to stay on watch for all of the forty-third to the forty-fifth nights, in order to be certain not to miss out on the main event. Antoine agreed to keep watch until one in the morning, at which time I took guard.

At about 4:30 on the morning of the forty-fourth day, the babies began to extricate themselves from the sand, as I lazily watched with my eyes half shut. Realizing what was happening, I ran to awaken Christine, Margaret, and Antoine. "They're hatching! They're hatching!" I proclaimed.

Within minutes, we were all at the beach watching the spectacle. The gradual process took several hours, but to our amazement, as the sun rose, so did the dangers to our newly-born friends.

At first, crabs began coming out of the sand, trying to grab the baby turtles and pull them to their holes. Then, seagulls came. Then dogs appeared, looking for an early morning breakfast. The challenge was before us. With the ferociousness of a mother hen safeguarding her chicks, we managed to protect every last turtle as they undertook their voyage to the sea. The four of us were continually on the move, scaring off predators.

By eight in the morning, the escapade was nearly over. All that remained were a half dozen late ones who seemed to be stunned into submission by the daylight.

"What if we get a bucket of salt water and place them in it for a couple of minutes? Maybe it'll wake them up," Christine suggested.

"I'll get a pail," I responded, while heading up to the lodge for a receptacle.

Sure enough, the gimmick worked. After two or three minutes in the water, the little things began to splash around, and upon release, they headed for the deep blue sea. We were all astonished at their ability to detect the direction of the ocean and follow their instinct to reach it. Without exception, they all found their way.

We estimated that eighty-six turtles made it to the ocean that morning. Very few would have succeeded, had it not been for our assistance.

It was a remarkable experience and we have never once regretted our forty-four days of waiting.

Within a few days, we departed on our journey to see Mexico. Although we did not manage to see the entire country in the five remaining months, we did see much of the southern and central portions. Fortunately, we have had occasion to return to extend our explorations.

CHAPTER 12

Where is Sibu?

After spending a month enjoying northern Thailand, we proceeded down Thailand's southern peninsula towards Malaysia. We had decided to make a two-month journey which would include a land trip to Singapore, followed by a flight to Indonesia. With the remaining time, we would visit Java and the more remote island of Flores, before returning to Bangkok. Travelers over the years had continually advised us that Flores was the most beautiful of the Indonesian islands with its abundant snorkeling, magnificent volcanoes, and Komodo dragons. On Java, we wanted to see Borobodur, reputed to be the largest Buddhist temple in Southeast Asia.

After lunch, we were walking towards the Hat Yai bus station in southern Thailand to catch a ride to Georgetown, Malaysia, when Christine went to purchase a newspaper."

Soon after, we were heading south towards the Malay border when I heard Christine ask, "Where is Sibu?"

"The only Cebu I know is spelled with a 'C' and is located in the central Philippines, somewhere in the Visaya Islands," I responded.

"This one starts with an 'S' and is spelled S I B U."

"I've never heard of it, but I can look it up in the *Rough Guide*. Why do you ask?"

"You can fly there for nineteen ringgits from Kuala Lumpur, which is about five dollars," she said.

"Sounds good. What airline offers such a deal?"

"Air Asia. I wonder where Sibu is located?"

I looked it up and within a few minutes, I had located Sibu in our guidebook. "It's an industrial port in Borneo. It doesn't sound like a very nice place."

"How about Kuching? You can fly there for twenty-nine ringgits," Christine stated.

After a bit more research, I responded, "It's also in Borneo, and it *does* sound like a nice place."

"How would you like to go to Borneo?" my traveling companion then asked.

"I've never considered it, but on the surface, it sounds good to me."

That evening, after settling into a guesthouse in Georgetown, we began to research the city of Kuching. We discovered that it is the capital of Sarawak, one of two Malaysian states located on the island of Borneo. The remainder of the large island is shared between Indonesia and Brunei.

Kuching rapidly became the focus of our research. Twenty-nine ringgits, or approximately eight dollars, was very appealing. However, Sarawak State and its capital became the real enticement.

First, we had to develop transportation plans that would work into our Indonesian trip. After a few minutes on the internet, Christine had us booked on a flight from Kuala Lumpur to Kuching. The flight would depart in fourteen days, which allowed us five days in the cool Cameron Highlands for some hiking, bird watching, and orchid gazing.

The remaining nine days would be spent taking in the sites of Kuala Lumpur, a city we had driven through several years hence but had never really visited.

Leaving Kuching was more complicated. We could return to Kuala Lumpur and then on to Java, but that second flight would be expensive. After a bit more reading, we discovered a suitable alternative that involved busing from Kuching to Pontianak, a port on the Indonesian portion of Borneo. From there, we could catch a ferry to Java for little money. The thirty-six-hour boat trip would be an interesting adventure and we looked forward to it.

Kuching ended up being more beautiful than the guidebook presented. We spent the better part of a month there, totally captivated by its enchanting people and jungle surroundings.

The historic port capital was very alluring. It had a riverfront park that created a nice setting for romantic evening strolls, enhanced by a glass of wine at one of the many cafés. The shopping among the city's many nooks and crannies allowed us to purchase an array of authentic tribal handicrafts. Good restaurants also abounded in the city, with a wide selection of ethnic cuisines. Being an old trading port, the city has a large Chinese community, an Indian population, many Malays, as well as a sprinkling of indigenous Dayaks. The mix is reflected in the diversity of architectural styles as well as foods.

A ten-minute boat ride across the river led us to an exquisite orchid garden. Christine and I concurred that among the many orchid gardens that we have visited, this was by far the most beautiful. Its riverfront setting, winding pathways, and gorgeous flowers made for a lovely day. The limited number of tourists was a bonus.

The next day, a short forty-five-minute bus drive found us at the Semenggok Wildlife Rehabilitation Center, where estranged orangutans are being prepared to reenter the wild. There are no cages or fences, as the animals are rehabilitated in a natural jungle environment. The orangutans are provided limited food once a day, as they prepare to venture out on their own. Visitors can hope to see them at mid-morning when they feed.

Our binoculars were essential, as the huge animals remained a significant distance from us and photography was limited due to the dark jungle cover. It was an amazing experience, watching the endangered species in their own environment. The Center is clearly set up for the convenience of the species, not the visitors. We were just distant spectators.

One afternoon, we visited the Sarawak Cultural Center, which provided an introduction to various native groups, as well as the architectural styles of their homes and villages. The Orang Ulu, Bidayuh, Iban, and Melanau are represented, as well as the intruding Chinese and Malays. The Center provided us with a sense of what life is like in the jungles. It also gave us a basis of information to help make decisions about further exploits inland. Our various conversations with people at the Center enlightened us to the fact that traveling inland amongst the indigenous people was safe.

Our two-month voyage to Indonesia from Thailand became a four-month adventure. We devoted half of the time between Malaysia proper and Borneo, followed by eight weeks in Indonesia as we had originally planned.

One of the lessons we have learned in our travels is to always remain flexible. Opportunities are plentiful for people who are able to take advantage of them when they arise. The best flight deals have often required that we make fast decisions, before the bargains are sold out. Our flexibility and ability to make a quick decision regarding the flight to Kuching is what enabled us to see and enjoy Borneo.

CHAPTER 13

Adventures at Bako National Park

We went to the Sarawak Tourist Association office in Kuching to book accommodations at Bako National Park. The lodging was owned and operated by the State of Sarawak and often booked to capacity, according to fellow travelers. Mistakenly, we only reserved for four nights, thinking that would allow us enough time to see the flora, fauna, and enjoy the parks and beaches. We soon discovered that a week or more would have been better. We tried to extend our stay, but to our dismay, there was no additional availability.

Bako is only twenty-five kilometers from Kuching, the capital of Sarawak State, on the island of Borneo. However, it seemed like an eternity away in terms of animals and vegetation. It is situated on a peninsula extending out into the South China Sea. Traveling there took us nearly an hour by bus to reach a small river harbor, and then another half hour with a fifteen-foot dingy. The variety of vegetation in this hilly area enables it to maintain an extensive array of wild animals.

We arrived mid-afternoon. After dropping off backpacks at our cabin, we decided to go for a refreshing swim. The water is always a nice respite in the heat of the tropics.

At sunset, we took a short jaunt along a trail that ran parallel to the ocean. To our amazement, just one kilometer from the cabin, we came across a bearded wild boar doing battle with a fallen coconut. He was utilizing a combination of his tusk and massive teeth to crush open the fruit to enjoy the meat. The process took fifteen minutes as Christine photographed the spectacle. The boar allowed us within fifteen feet before warning us off with a loud grunt. Needless to say, we maintained our distance. Neither of us had ever seen a two-hundred-pound bearded pig in the wild, so we marveled at the sight.

One half kilometer further, we came upon a troop of endangered proboscis monkeys. The rare creatures descend from the jungles in early evening to dine on the tender coastal vegetation. We encountered nearly a dozen of these long-nosed animals over the next half hour. Had the darkness not engulfed us, we may have watched for hours. Binoculars were much in order, as the monkeys are not particularly fond of humans.

After this experience, we found it advantageous to always carry binoculars and our camera while hiking the area, for we never knew what animal, bird, or unique plant was lurking around the bend.

The next day after breakfast, we began our hike along the Telok Pandan Trail to remote Kecil Beach. Before setting off, we made arrangements for a local boatman to pick us up at the beach at 3 p.m. for a quick ride back. That would provide us ample time to enjoy both the hike and the beach. Had we not arranged the pick-up, we would have spent most of the day hiking back and forth.

Walking along the trail, not far from our lodge, we encountered a group of silver haired monkeys. There must have been at least twenty of the brave creatures. They seemed very accustomed to humans, as they approached for food.

Having no handouts available, we simply took photographs of the young scooting about.

Our trail soon had us climbing some rather steep and rough terrain which took us inland to an elevated plateau. Within a half hour, we had encountered three different vegetation zones. Though we are not botanists by any means, we were able to detect and photograph the strange pitcher-like plants that have lids which close in on unsuspecting insects. The foreign guest is then digested in the soupy liquid contained within the strange plant. This species was different in shape and size from the famed Venus flytrap. We had never seen any plant like it before.

After a long walk and a brief rain shower, we found ourselves looking down a three-hundred-foot cliff at Kecil Beach. I still marvel at the descent when thinking about it. The hazardous trek down took more than half an hour, but was well worth the effort. We are not rock climbers and this descent was difficult for novices.

Kecil Beach is a small cove surrounded on three sides by steep rock cliffs and open to the ocean on the fourth side. One of its main features is a small stream that flows down from the plateau above and runs into the sea. The gentle waves make for excellent swimming. We had been warned of jellyfish with dangerous stings, but there were none to be found on this particular day.

There were no other people at the beach, which made the experience all the more special. After the brief morning shower, the sun was upon us, and by mid-afternoon, we found ourselves seeking shade from the encroaching cliffs.

While I went for a swim, Christine stated that she would follow the stream into the canyon as far as she could. Within a few minutes, she returned exclaiming, "Come and see!

There are little fish skipping above the water and onto the land. They're really cute. You should see them."

Within minutes, we were observing hundreds of mudskippers as they traversed the stream onto the sandy shoreline. We enjoyed watching the two-inch long skippers meander about in search of food.

Before long, the boatman picked us up as arranged. The trip back along the rocky coast was reminiscent of the rugged Maine coast. It ended the day on a beautiful note.

The next morning provided us with the most engaging animal experience of our stay at Bako. A troop of macaque monkeys were all around our cabin making an abundance of noise and rousting us out of bed. They were under the floor and on the roof and porch.

Later, while Christine was at the Canteen procuring a cup of coffee and I was busy photographing a young monkey, I heard a loud noise come from inside the cabin. Turning, I noticed a screen had been opened. As I quickly began running towards the cabin, a mischievous gray-haired monkey ran through the open window with one of my shirts in hand. Not to be outdone, I chased it behind the building, and much to my relief, he surrendered his recent acquisition as he scooted up a banyan tree. We had been warned about the thieves and had now experienced them firsthand. Henceforth, we kept both windows and doors locked.

The most elusive wild animals in the park are the nocturnal cats called civets. With a long, striped tail, they slowly meander about the elevated tree limbs in search of fruit. Returning from dinner one evening, we saw a local man flashing his spotlight in the tree.

"What are you looking for?" I asked.

"The little cat," he responded in broken English. "Come along," he added.

With the eyes of an eagle, the man soon spotted two of these night wanderers and guided our eyes to these rare felines. Without his assistance, we would have never seen nor even known these creatures were in the vicinity. The same gentleman then guided us to a bush lit up with fireflies. It was like a Christmas tree lit up for our viewing pleasure.

Over the next couple of days, we wandered along other trails in the park and made a return journey to Kecil Beach, which was our favorite. As previously mentioned, four days was too little time for the wonders of this place. If ever we come back to Borneo, we will certainly return to Bako National Park.

CHAPTER 14

The Biggest Flowers in the World

Every day, we stopped in at the Sarawak Tourism Association office to check on the status of the Rafflesia flowers, reputed to be the biggest flowers in the world. If and when one was to bloom, we were determined to see it.

The flower's reputation as the largest flower comes from measurements up to three feet across and up to fifteen pounds, though often much less. They are a reddish-brown color with a rubbery substance inside which attracts insects into their depths. The flowers grow in dense jungle forests which make them very difficult to locate. They only bloom for a couple of days per year, so it is essential to view them as quickly as possible if opportunity arises. In conjunction with Gunung Gading National Park, the tourist bureau monitors the situation and advices travelers when a specimen has reached its zenith.

On our fifth visit to the tourist office, we noticed a photograph of a Rafflesia on the computer screen, which indicated that we were in luck. The helpful tourist attendant recognized us, and with a smile, told us that two had opened during the past twenty-four hours. They were both at Gunung Gading. We thanked her profusely and decided to head to the park the next morning.

At eight the next day, we boarded a local bus for a jostling two-and-a-half-hour ride to the town of Lundu. From there, we employed a small van to transport us to the national park, which is at the southern end of Sarawak.

From the park headquarters, a friendly guide led us through dense jungle, via a rugged, wet trail to the flowers. The mud we sloshed through had us slipping and sliding. The most difficult part was crossing a raging river by jumping from rock to rock. However, the climactic end made the venture worth the effort.

It seemed a bit extreme to have a guide lead us to two flowers, but the blooms would otherwise be impossible to locate in the dense growth of Borneo. The park provided and required the companion, not only for directional guidance, but also to protect these rare flowers, as there have been thieves who have tried to steal the emerging plants.

After our short ride back to Lundu, we found ourselves with over two hours to spend in this small town. I checked our guidebook to see what it said about the place and read aloud, "Lundu is a pleasant enough town, but there is nothing to keep you here."

"I saw pepper plantations all around," Christine responded. "Maybe we can purchase some fresh pepper. We can put it in nice bottles and give it away as authentic gifts from Borneo."

With an abundance of pepper plantations in the area, I applauded her idea, feeling confident about the ease in locating fresh pepper to buy. We only needed one pound of the peppercorns, which we would later repackage in glass cylinders.

We began our stroll around the three-block village. Finding establishments selling pepper was simple enough, as there were several shops selling the commodity. However, it was rather challenging to purchase it in a relatively small quantity. They all sold both white and black whole peppercorns, but in twenty-five-kilogram burlap bags (about fifty pounds). The dealers would not budge from this minimum sale.

Finally, after having covered the entire town, we located one kind wholesaler who gave in. Not only did he agree to sell us the mere one-kilogram quantity, he was also nice enough to break it down into half black and half white peppercorns.

Accomplishing this simple task brought us joy. We achieved what seemed to be the impossible. We laughed at the thought of possibly not being able to buy pepper in the midst of all these plantations. If this had been in the west, the town would have been covered with tourist stands selling the product in pretty packages at atrocious prices.

Reveling in our accomplishment, we sat down in a dusty little restaurant for lunch. Christine ordered an omelet and I enjoyed a delicious dish of vegetable fried rice. When the food was placed on the table, Christine looked around and asked, "Where's the pepper?"

There was no pepper, and here we were in pepper heaven. When I asked the waitress for pepper, she merely shrugged. We enjoyed our meal, even without pepper, then caught the bus to Kuching.

On the ride back, we marveled at another wondrous day, during which we had seen a sample of the world's largest and possibly smelliest flower in its natural habitat, and also managed to buy pepper under very adverse conditions. The marvels of travel never cease to amaze and entrance us. Simple things often make for quite a fine day.

CHAPTER 15

Waving to a Policeman

Ubud, a small city in South Central Bali, is one of the more delightful places we have visited. It is one of those towns you go to with the intention to stay a few days, but could end up spending a week or possibly even a month. Albeit touristy, it maintains the charm of a bygone era, with the modernity of the twenty-first century.

There is a broad selection of accommodations in a wide price range. Homestays are very reasonable and provide an excellent means of meeting locals. With so many to choose from, we had no difficulty finding a very comfortable setting that overlooked a rice paddy. Living within the family compound enabled us to make friends and familiarize ourselves with daily routines.

The multi-cultural cuisine of the city is worth sampling. We found it to be most pleasing to the palate. One of our favorite restaurants overlooks bright green rice paddies with towering coconut trees in the background. The quacking of ducks splashing through the paddies is a welcome addition to the scenery. For those on a budget, which we are most of the time, there is always the neighborhood *warung,* small, family-owned restaurant serving up delicious meals at reasonable prices.

Our homestay also rented out bicycles, which I utilized on a daily basis. Small cities like Ubud are easy to maneuver about on a bike and are a lovely way to visit neighboring villages while meandering through the rice-field-enriched countryside. On many afternoons, I would break away for an hour or two and enjoy the magnificence of the island on my two-wheeler.

Ubud is often called the cultural center of Bali, and justly so. A host of activities abound throughout the vicinity, particularly in the evening. Kecak dances with the rhythmic beating of sticks and fire walking is just one of the indigenous forms of entertainment. Puppet shows and gamelan music can also be enjoyed on most evenings. The venues vary tremendously and provide a constant source of entertainment.

Our homestay family invited us to join them for the funeral of a dignitary. We accepted and even joined in on the procession to the cremation site. Balinese are often Hindu and believe the spirit does not leave the body until the latter is cremated. Hence, the funeral is an extravagant and costly affair. With much music and ceremony, we marched to the funerary site. The body of the deceased was wrapped in cloth and placed in a massive horned bull made of plaster and paper. At the end of the procession, the bull containing the body was placed on a large pile of wood and at the appropriate moment, set ablaze with the aid of gasoline. Hundreds of people looked on, as the deceased was evidently well-liked and respected.

On our last trip to Bali, we noticed that tickets were being sold to tourists for attending cremation ceremonies. Upon investigation, we found that it is not necessary to buy a ticket, as an invitation will do. It is indeed unfortunate that such a serious event as a funeral has been reduced to that of a tourist spectacle. Although tourism dollars benefit the economy of a region, it is disheartening to observe the culture of local inhabitants being so compromised.

We became friendly with Ketut, a young waitress who seemed to enjoy our company. On one occasion, she invited us to join her and her boyfriend, Wayan, as well as a couple of other friends, on a Sunday afternoon excursion to Besakih Temple on Mount Agung. The mountain is the largest of all the volcanic peaks on the island and is the site of several Hindu temples, the combination of which is called Besakih. Every twelve years, a month-long series of ceremonies takes place at a village temple located within this massive complex. All villages on the island have a temple on the mountain, and all its citizens attempt to participate in one of the ceremonies during this special month.

Christine and I just happened to be in Bali during this special time and were more than happy to accept Ketut's invitation. We rented a vehicle, and Wayan, who was a professional tour guide, made all the arrangements for our excursion.

At 10 a.m., we met up with our escort and her many friends. How we all managed to fit into that small jeep is still beyond my comprehension, but somehow, all ten of us made it into a vehicle designed for four passengers. It appeared to be a come one, come all invitation with Ketut and her entourage. Before embarking on our journey, Ketut saw to it that we were both dressed from head to foot in typical Balinese ceremonial attire. Christine was dressed with a lovely sarong and embroidered blouse. I wore a sarong, formal jacket, and turban-style headdress. It made us feel good to be taken in, and enabled us to better fit in with the crowd.

Wayan took an elongated route around the eastern end of the island, providing us with commentary when appropriate. The winding roads brought us through rice paddies, over mountains, and through many small villages. Although a bit crowded, we had a wonderful time viewing the surroundings and enjoying the company of these congenial people.

Reaching the temple complex amongst thousands of locals, Ketut led us to the particular temple of her home village. Joining in with other pilgrims, we received a blessing from the Hindu cleric, being dignified with blessed water and sanctified rice. We were honored to participate and thankful for the opportunity to share this religious experience with the Balinese.

As well-known as the ceremony was, and with its numerous participants, we saw absolutely no westerners at Besakih that day. We were treated by the residents like locals, and felt comfortable sharing this holy event with them on Mount Agung. We felt as if we were one with them, and that was a very good feeling.

It would be impossible to talk about Ubud and not mention shopping. The town and surrounding villages have hundreds, if not thousands, of shops lining the streets. Browsing through art galleries, woodcarver's shops, antique stores, and clothing boutiques could keep one occupied for months. I was nearly shopped-out when Christine said, "Let's rent a motorbike and shop in some of the adjoining communities," to which I hesitatingly agreed.

We rarely rent motorbikes and may even be a bit aged for the adventure, but it was enticing to head out to areas with limited traffic and minimal population. Our goal was to get going early in the morning. We would travel over the mountains to the north side of the island and make the return journey later that day, stopping here and there for shopping and sightseeing.

The designated day was sunny and pleasant. By 7:30, we were on our way. We stopped at several craft and gift shops in the morning, but did not buy anything on our way north, as we planned to stop at select stores for our purchases on the return journey.

The variety of woodworking alone was amazing. Signs, masks, kitchen utensils, and statues were all hand-carved.

We received a surprise as we crossed the apex of the mountains, preparing to descend down the northern slope. Bali is a tropical island just south of the equator and always quite warm, that is unless you are crossing mountains on a motorbike. Wearing short-sleeved shirts, we were not prepared for the cool mountaintop air. In fact, we froze while circumventing the summit of a volcano. Needless to say, the descent on the opposite side was most welcome. It would have been simple enough to carry extra layers with us, had we anticipated the weather conditions. It is too easy to forget the dramatic impact elevation has on temperature.

Indonesian police are notorious for taking bribes from tourists. In fact, it is not uncommon to hear travelers complain of being stopped by a policeman, bogusly charged with running a red light, and finding that all is forgiven after paying an on-the-spot fine. Knowing this, we were careful to follow all of the designated rules of the road while driving across the island. Christine would caution, "Slow down," or, "Red light ahead."

It was no surprise when Christine nudged me from the back and stated, "Stop sign ahead." Dutifully, I stopped, looked both ways, and began to drive off when I heard a whistle blow. About one hundred fifty feet to our right, I observed a policeman, whistle in mouth, waving me over.

There are many times in life when I have chided myself for not thinking or reacting fast enough. Sometimes thinking—I should have done it this way instead of that. However, this time, I quickly appraised the situation for what it was: the policeman intended to bribe us. I noticed that he was on foot with no car or motorcycle. He was a lone policeman, dropped off, and assigned to this particular intersection. With no more than a quick look in his direction, I waved back to him, as if to say hello, then quickly sped off. He was left with nothing to do but watch as his potential bribe drove away.

Our return to Ubud that day was uneventful, although we did stop here and there for an occasional purchase. Limited to what we could buy due to the motorbikes, we rented an automobile on a subsequent day, for an additional shopping spree.

We enjoyed our two weeks in Ubud, always managing to keep busy. A combination of marvelous sights, great shopping, and lovely people make it a wonderful place to visit. We have returned on several occasions, always regaling our tale of the waving policeman.

CHAPTER 16

Free Camping in New Zealand

We flew into Christchurch on South Island, New Zealand on May 21st, which was late fall for the islanders. We allocated three weeks for visiting the country, planning to spend half of our time on the South Island and the other half on the North Island. Guidebooks and fellow travelers had suggested busing, but one article we read mentioned renting a camper as a means of transportation and lodging.

"Let's look into it when we get to the airport," Christine said, referring to renting a camper van.

Although I heard her, I did not really expect we could afford it. "Okay, it's the off-season. Maybe we can find some good rates."

The time of year as well as the fierce competition worked to our advantage. We arrived at the airport mid-day and found two competitive camper rental agencies directly across from one another within a small lounge area. We set down our luggage and Christine called a backpacker lodge to make reservations for the night. When they asked what time we would like to be picked up at the airport, she wisely responded, "We'll call you back in a little while."

Knowing we had time on our hands and no other travelers to compete with, we began our negotiations for a camper van, as New Zealanders call them.

I went to the first agency and came back saying, "Sixty New Zealand dollars per day with unlimited miles," then added, "Way too much."

Christine agreed and suggested I try the other rental operation.

Waiting for the moment when I was certain the first agent was watching, I went to the second group. Within a few minutes, I returned to Christine and said, "Fifty-five and unlimited miles."

"We have to do better than that. Maybe we ought to use the buses."

"Maybe," I responded, "but let's play around here for a while. I don't think these people are being overwhelmed by customers," I facetiously noted.

At this point, the airport was empty except for a few employees. For the next hour, we went back and forth until an agency lowered its price to forty-five NZ dollars per day (about $30 U.S.) with unlimited miles. We would have to pay for the fuel, but the vehicle had a diesel engine and in this environmentally friendly country, diesel fuel was sixty percent the cost of regular gas. In addition, we soon discovered the vehicle consumed very little fuel.

The camper van provided transport, sleeping quarters, and a kitchen, for what we considered a reasonable price. The first night in New Zealand, we slept at a lodge and ate at a restaurant. For the next three weeks, we lived exclusively in the van. Fortunately for us, Christine is an excellent cook and we ate better than restaurants could have ever provided.

The morning after we made the arrangements, we went to the Automobile Association for an assortment of maps and travel advice. We then picked up some cold weather clothing at the local Goodwill Store. Our ten months of traveling this particular year was exclusively in tropical climates, except for New Zealand, so we were ill-prepared for the chilly temperature. Once equipped, we picked up our rental and were off to see New Zealand.

The AA office had kindly told us that we could *free camp* in this country which meant we could park anywhere we wanted unless there was a sign specifically prohibiting camping. They also reassured us that it was safe to camp anywhere. This allowed us to select overnight locations with spectacular views. Our first night was no exception as we selected a site overlooking a beautiful aqua blue lake with Mount Cook and the Southern Alps as a backdrop. The next morning, we simply rolled back the curtains in our warm, cozy van and enjoyed the view. Over the next few weeks, we bedded down and arose to beautiful sunsets, sunrises, mirror lakes, glaciers, and ocean views. It was like heaven on earth. Our only limitation was that every few nights, we had to overnight at a campground in order to recharge the batteries and fill the van with water.

Over the years, fellow travelers, friends, and relatives have asked us to name the most beautiful places we have visited. The South Island of New Zealand is always on our list. Over the one and a half weeks, we were continually blessed with a variety of great scenery. One minute it was Pancake Rocks, the next, some snow-capped rolling hills, then herds of deer...

The hot springs and geysers of the North Island also abounded with scenic beauty. Over a three-day period in the Rotorua area, we visited Maoris, glowworm caves, and primeval settings while returning to relaxing evenings in the sizzling waters of a local hot spring.

To add to our enjoyment, we noticed an ad in the local paper promoting wild game meat. Without hesitation, we headed to the store located on the site of the processing plant. Fortunately, our van was equipped with a small refrigerator freezer so we were able to build an inventory of wild boar, venison, and hare. Although we had limited facilities, Christine was able to cook up some memorable and delicious meals.

We were able to drop the camper van off at the Auckland Airport, which was very convenient. Being able to fly onto one island and depart from the other saved significant time. Unfortunately, with only three weeks, we didn't get further north than Auckland on the North Island. I suppose this gives us an excuse to return. We would likely take advantage of the free camping again, as this nation offers jaw-dropping beauty at every bend.

CHAPTER 17

A Flight Over the Nazca Lines

Christine and I were drawn to Nazca because of the mystique surrounding the lines. All the literature we had read strongly suggested seeing this phenomenon from the air in order to appreciate it in its full glory. It is the only way of viewing the lines in their entirety. We have read *National Geographic* articles about Nazca along with the Von Daniken book, which suggests that the lines were the creation of aliens. All of the reading emphasized the advantage of aerial viewing, so that was our plan.

Our first sense of the immensity of the Nazca lines came when we visited Le Museo de la Nation in Lima, Peru. Massive dioramas and photographs along with artifacts began to develop the setting and prepare us for seeing them. The museum also helped us realize the enormous number of archeological sites in Peru. I had a fixation that the Incas had been the empire of Peru but in reality, they were merely one of many. Other great civilizations existed prior to the Incas. The extremely arid coastline of Peru abounds in relics of pre-Inca groups.

In seeing the archeological evidence preserved by the desert, I wondered what else existed in ancient times, perhaps in other parts of the world, where climatic conditions do not naturally preserve? How much has been lost? Were the civilizations of old much more advanced than remains indicate? How much has been wasted away in tropical or semi-tropical climates with the passage of time? Our visit to the Museo de la Nation opened up our eyes to what we may not know about the ancient civilizations of the world. The museum had accomplished what great museums should: to pose as many questions as it answers.

We caught a night bus for the eight-hour journey from Lima to the town of Nazca. To our surprise, Nazca is a very small city set in the midst of a large desert. We had expected a much grander place because of its international fame. We concluded that although the town attracts many tourists, most only stay for a short time. We stayed for several days, but most visitors remain just one night—see the lines, then move on.

After a short nap the next morning, the desk clerk at our hotel suggested that we visit the Nazca Museum, prior to flying over the area. He said that it was small and not well known, yet told the story of the lines very well.

Too tired to take on the museum after the all-night ride, we decided to simply stroll around town. The market and shops were similar to other small, South American villages. It had the usual assortment of fruits, vegetables, and household items one expects, but no traveler-related gifts. Those were strictly found in the immediate vicinity of the large hotels. Some restaurants had menus slanted for tourists, though most were for locals. The few gringos we did see were in restaurants, not on the streets.

On our second day, we made our way to the Nazca Museum. Although a bit difficult to find and a good distance from the center of town, it was well worth the effort. It was by no means crowded as we were its only visitors, yet we found it to be a treasure of information. We discovered that Von Daniken was only one of a string of people who had studied the lines since they had been rediscovered, and that theories abound regarding their purpose. We also found that large portions of this desert area were eroded from heavy rains one thousand years ago, though most of the lines remain intact.

Once again, we found ourselves asking more questions. Were there other lines in other parts of the world that have not been discovered or preserved? Maybe buried in the depths of some jungle?

On our third day, after a light breakfast, we caught a taxi to the airport. This in itself was a luxury for us, as we normally use local bus transportation. At the airport, we found ourselves sharing the shade of a huge tree with a llama. With a coke and coffee in hand, we waited for about an hour for the winds to die down in order for the plane to take off.

Finally, we boarded the small plane and began our one-hour flight. The imposing size of what we observed is almost beyond belief. The length and width are such that it took us fifteen minutes by plane to traverse the valley that contains the lines. We had read about some of the lines forming a monkey and hummingbird, but the sight of the enormous designs was far beyond our expectations.

Christine clicked away with the camera as we flew over sight after sight. We were fortunate to be flying on a clear day.

Returning to the ground, we thanked the pilot profusely for the flight and commentary. Once again, we had experienced one of the wonders of the world and were most appreciative. Although there are observation stands from which to view the lines, we would strongly recommend a flight to fully appreciate their immensity and magnificence.

Flying over the Nazca Lines was well worthwhile and provided us with another fulfilling day. To this day, we are in awe.

CHAPTER 18

Don't Eat the Lettuce

Arequipa is a beautiful city set on the lower slopes of the Andes Mountains in southern Peru. The six thousand feet of elevation take it out of the coastal desert heat, yet it is considerably warmer than the frigid heights of Puno and Lake Titicaca at fourteen thousand feet. The low humidity and mild temperatures are perfect for walking.

Once we arrived, we immediately set out to see the sites of interest since we only planned to spend a couple of days here. The centuries old convent in the center of town is a preserved piece of Spanish colonial architecture. The picture-perfect walking lanes amongst chapels, dormitories, and working quarters add to the aura of this grand city. Getting lost within this massive compound as we strolled along made it all the more enjoyable.

The following morning, we began our exploits in search of alpaca material. Not knowing precisely what we were going to use the fabric for, we set out in pursuit of the perfect piece at a reasonable price.

"Now is the time to buy, while we're in Peru," Christine stated as our search ensued. "This is where they raise alpaca."

I could not challenge the validity of making our purchase in this country, though I did wonder the point of our endeavor if we had no particular purpose for it. Nevertheless,

I went along and enjoyed the quest as we meandered about the city.

We ventured from one store to another and finally, by late afternoon, in a small shop packed with materials, Christine found what she wanted. It was a dark, navy-blue color and as soft as one could imagine. Many of the alpaca cloths we located in Peru featured overly ornate designs or boring colors, so finding the navy was much more difficult than one might think.

Two years hence, I must admit that the material has made a very handsome sports jacket that I proudly wear on special occasions. Being well-lined and made of pure alpaca wool, it is not only beautiful but also appreciated in cold weather.

Walking a couple of kilometers back to our guesthouse, we found that we had worked up an appetite. "Let's stop and have an early dinner," I suggested.

Christine was agreeable and we decided on a restaurant whose specialty was rotisserie chicken.

The eatery had a very limited menu. Rotisserie chicken with either fried potatoes or salad was the extent of it. Forgetting one of the golden rules of travel in South America, *Don't eat the lettuce*, I ordered the poultry dish with salad. Christine wisely opted for the potatoes.

We enjoyed our simple lunch, but I began to feel the effects around two the following morning. I awoke and began tossing and turning with extreme stomach discomfort. Unintentionally, I woke Christine and she suggested an Alka Seltzer. Unfortunately, it did nothing to alleviate the situation. In fact, by 3 a.m., it was clear my condition was getting worse.

My wife went to see if the desk clerk could assist us in locating a medical doctor. Fortunately, an employee was on duty. Many guesthouses close up after midnight with no attendees.

Within a few minutes, Christine returned stating that there was a hospital three blocks away and the desk clerk was out hailing a taxi. Once again, luck was with me as Arequipa is a large enough city to keep cabs running all night. Walking the short distance to the hospital would have been nearly impossible at this stage of my illness.

By the time we were out of the building, the clerk had a taxi waiting, and within a few minutes, we found ourselves arriving at the hospital.

We got to the emergency room and although our Spanish is limited, Christine was able to explain my situation as I solemnly waited.

Upon return, she said, "I have to go pay the hospital fee before the doctor will see you."

A bit folded over in discomfort, I knew there was no point in fighting bureaucracy. "Okay," I responded, and continued to wait.

Twenty minutes later, with receipt in hand, she returned, explaining that the line was slow-moving.

Showing the receipt to the nurse, we were told to sit and wait. The doctor would see me in turn.

Thankfully, within minutes, the physician called us in and after several questions, she diagnosed me with having food poisoning. She then added, in perfect English, that in order to be certain, I would need several laboratory tests.

"Thank you," I said, and asked for directions to the lab.

Arriving at the laboratory, Christine provided the attendant with the written instructions. Looking at the paper he told her, "You have to pay the lab fee before I can do the tests."

Off again, she went to wait in the long, slow line to pay the fee, returning twenty minutes later.

In a very efficient manner, the technician took the test and within half an hour, we had the results in writing for the doctor.

While we were waiting, I explained my situation and the physician's diagnosis to a man sitting near me. Upon departure, he looked at me, and with a smile on his face, he bid me farewell and advised for future reference, "Don't eat the lettuce."

Back to the main office with lab results in hand, we were told we would have to pay another fee before the doctor could see me again. What felt like an hour later, Christine returned from the now familiar line.

Soon after, we were with the physician. With written confirmation of food poisoning, she wrote out two prescriptions. One of the medications was a strong antibiotic and the other for electrolytes to rebuild my fluids.

"Is there somewhere we can get these filled at this time of morning?" Christine asked.

"The hospital pharmacy is open," the doctor responded. "Just go down the corridor and turn left."

"Thank you for seeing me," I said. "I hope I don't have to see you again."

"You'll be okay," she said. "Just don't eat the lettuce."

We headed directly to the pharmacy. Handing over the prescriptions to the pharmacist, she reviewed them and said, "You have to pay before I can give you the medications."

"Where do we pay?" Christine dejectedly asked, knowing all too well she was heading back to the dreaded line.

Twenty minutes later, I was taking the medications and within the hour, I was well on my way to recovery. I profusely thanked Christine for waiting in those lines four times. "I could never have done it without you."

I later observed her clicking away on the calculator and asked what she was working on.

"Just adding up the total cost of the medical care," she replied.

"How much was it?"

"Hospital, doctor, lab, and pharmacy came to four dollars and twenty-five cents," she responded. "If only we could have paid for it all at once."

The care, diagnosis, and treatment I received were excellent. However, the time that elapsed while we were at the hospital was long and tiresome. That was the Peruvian way of doing things, and I was appreciative of their assistance. And I certainly couldn't complain about the expense.

Our stay in Arequipa was extended for several days as I regained my strength. We knew the bus ride to Puno would be long and we were aware that the climb to the upper Andes would take adjusting to and could possibly cause altitude sickness.

"There is one lesson from this," I said to my wife as we left Araquipa.

"What is that?"

"Don't eat the lettuce."

CHAPTER 19

The Mysterious Tea

The all-day bus ride from Arequipa to Puno was a spectacular voyage to the upper reaches of the Andean Range. The semi-arid plains were frequented by herds of llamas and occasional alpacas. The beauty of the treeless Altiplano stood in stark contrast to the summits and ridges of the ranges to the east. The bus provided a far superior means of transportation over flying due to the scenery.

We had called in advance for reservations at a small hotel in downtown Puno. The young Peruvian voice on the phone stated that his father would pick us up at the bus station at the appointed time of arrival. However, our bus was running two hours late and would arrive at midnight instead of 10 p.m. Being that late, we did not anticipate that they would still be waiting, but low and behold, Juan and his wife Paulina were there, looking cheerful and holding a sign welcoming Christine and Richard in big bold letters. We greeted them with thankful handshakes. Unfortunately, their warm welcome was no indication of the frigid Puno air. We quickly dug into our backpacks for sweaters and hats.

Within a half hour, Juan showed us to our master room on the fourth floor of his homey hotel. Like other low to mid-range hotels in the area, we did not have heat in our room, so we soon found ourselves under a bundle of comfortable blankets. Snuggling together, we quickly fell asleep after the long bus ride.

Prior to leaving the warmth of the bed on the following morning, Christine mentioned that she had a headache and an uneasy stomach.

"That's strange," I said. "I also have a slight headache. I'll get a couple of aspirins. That should help."

"Maybe we can get some breakfast?" she suggested. On our way to the restaurant, she asked, "Do you think it could be altitude sickness?"

"I don't know, but there is a *farmacia* straight ahead. Let's stop and ask for their advice."

"Anything is worth a try. My head is killing me," my wife stated while we headed straight for the apothecary.

The young lady behind the counter agreed with our diagnosis and gave us medication with the added comment, "There is no real cure. It will take a few days to get acclimated."

After breakfast, we walked around the town center. The shops were of interest, but Christine's persistent headache put a damper on the day, so we decided to return to the hotel for rest.

Guidebooks suggest taking it easy for the first few days if affected by altitude. Although the impact on me was minor, Christine felt seriously ill.

Upon entering the lobby of our hotel, Juan greeted us and asked us how we were enjoying Puno. A bit dejected, we explained our situation and told him we bought medication and would rest.

Using his son as an interpreter, he asked to see the medicine. After seeing it, he developed a smile and in a commanding voice, he stated, "This won't work."

"Should we be chewing on coca leaves?" I asked. Many travelers had advised us to chew coca leaves when above twelve thousand feet, suggesting it would alleviate the symptoms. Coca leaves could be found in all the markets and we were game to try anything, especially after Juan told us that the pharmacy medication would not help.

"Coca leaves are only so-so," Alverez translated from his father.

"What else can we do?" asked Christine.

"My dad will get some tea for you. Just drink four to six cups per day and you will feel much better by tomorrow. It is like magic."

"Can we buy the tea from you?" I asked, hoping to move the process along.

"You just go upstairs and my dad will be there in a few minutes."

By this stage in our travels, Christine and I had learned not to shrug off home remedies. People of remote places, like the Altiplano, had discovered cures over the centuries that would never be acceptable by western standards. Yet, many of their methods had worked for them and their ancestors time and again over hundreds of years.

In less than five minutes, Juan was at our door with a huge thermos full of his homemade tea concoction. Thus began a remarkable recovery.

By evening, we went out to dinner, though still a bit under the weather. Fortunately, we were not on a rigid schedule, so we hung around town for several extra days to fully recover.

Chatting with Juan and some of his associates during our stay, we learned that he was an economist who had forgone his position as an economics professor for the greener pastures of hotel ownership. Among his university colleagues, we were surprised to find others preparing to make a similar move in life. I found it interesting that these well-educated people continued to respect the past, as exemplified by the homemade remedy.

Within two days, we visited the famed Floating Islands on Lake Titicaca and soon found ourselves hiking along a fifteen-kilometer trail over the beautiful hills and dales of Isle del Sol. Clearly, the tea had worked its wonders.

Thanks to Juan and his mysterious tea, we were prepared to move south and take on the even higher elevations of Bolivia.

CHAPTER 20

The Stolen Camera

The bus ride to La Paz, Bolivia was beautiful as we could see the towering peaks of the snowcapped Andes off to our left. The second level of the first class *Ormano* bus provided excellent views with its wrap-around windows.

Our delayed border crossing between Peru and Bolivia afforded us an interesting insight in the ways of South America. Disembarking from the bus, a young boy approached Christine saying, "Follow me. No lines. Let me help you."

Feeling somewhat daring, we followed the youngster between cars, crowds, and through a market until we reached a Peruvian immigration checkout station. It was the only checkpoint with no lines. While following the boy, we had observed several immigration lines of twenty to thirty people waiting for their departure stamp.

Before getting stamped, Christine thoughtfully asked the boy, "How much?" knowing the young fellow had not directed us here out of his empathy for gringos.

He only asked for the equivalent of twenty-five cents, and he added that the price included Bolivian immigration.

We paid him and in less than two minutes, we had our Peruvian exit stamp and our Bolivian entrance procedure was just as quick and easy with the assistance of our young friend.

When leaving our escort we gave him a tip, and with a broad grin on his face, he directed us back to our waiting vehicle. We found the bus devoid of people and upon quick examination, we realized that our fellow passengers were still in line waiting for their exit stamps. We ended up waiting another two hours for them to make their way through immigration.

The drive from the border on the high plains of Bolivia was stunning with the sterile cropped grass of the Altiplano slopes backed by range upon range of mountains. Within a couple of hours, we found ourselves arriving at the La Paz bus station. Colorful bands and dancing locals in bright costumes encircled the area as we arrived in the midst of a fiesta. Hoping to later get a glimpse of the festivities, we quickly made our way into the station.

We had been warned to keep a close watch on our bags at the La Paz station as the place abounds with thieves waiting for innocent travelers. We set our four bags down on a bench, about ten feet from a phone booth. I stood hovering above them as Christine went to the booth to call the guesthouse.

A minute after my wife stepped away, a man approached me from my right and said "Ormano?" the name of the bus company from which we had departed. I looked at him but then quickly realized I was being set-up. I checked the bags and found that one of our small carry bags had been stolen. A second person working in tandem had taken it.

Unbeknownst to me, at the very moment I was being robbed, a third person had approached Christine from the opposite direction while she was making the phone call, saying "Ormano?" to distract her attention as she too had a full view of our bags.

A run around the station and notifying the police accomplished nothing. "What was in the missing bag?" I asked Christine upon returning from my jaunt.

"The camera, all our cold weather clothing, and my Pashmina scarf from Nepal," she responded.

It was a dejecting experience to say the least. The clothing proved easy to replace at a local goodwill store, but the camera was of excellent quality and very reliable. Replacing it would be more difficult. The authentic scarf we would not be able to replace unless we returned to Nepal, and hence was considered a lost cause.

Our first attempt to replace the camera was to locate the thieves' market. We had been so pleased with our camera that we thought we would buy it back, if we could locate it. Several trips to the looters' area proved fruitless. One vendor thought that it would likely not appear for a couple of weeks.

After several days, we found ourselves planning to head south to the Uyuni Salt Flats and Lagunas Colorada. As these were reputed to be the most photogenic areas in all of Bolivia, purchasing a new camera was necessary. We invested in the new piece of equipment and proceeded south. After six hours on a bus ride and an overnight twelve-hour train journey, we found ourselves in the desolate town of Uyuni. The place reminded us of a dusty, non-descript American Western town from the late eighteen hundreds. "The Dodge City of Bolivia," I commented to my wife.

With not much to see in the town, we quickly boarded a four-wheel jeep for one of the most photo-worthy, fascinating, and frigid exploits of our traveling years. Amidst the snow-covered peaks were gorgeous colored lakes of vivid reds and greens, swirling as the bright sun and brisk winds reflected on them. Steamy geysers, llamas, alpacas, and dirt encrusted villages added to the drama of our four-day adventure.

Our only disappointment was that our new camera stopped operating while we explored this wonderland. Fortunately, a third traveler had joined us for the trip; he was kind enough to send us replacement photos upon his return to Belgium.

When we returned to La Paz, we went back to the thieves' market in search of our stolen camera, but had no luck.

"We have to go back to the shop that sold us this camera and get it replaced," Christine stated.

Much to our amazement, the owner of the camera store allowed us a new, upgraded camera at very minimal cost.

Happily, we were on our way south with our new camera, to Machu Picchu and the Galapagos Islands. However, to our dismay, the second new camera was as defective as the first. The jinx of the stolen camera was still with us. Although the second new camera held up better than the first by providing us great photographs of Machu Picchu, it failed us in the Galapagos Islands. Needless to say, there were no repair shops when we needed one. Once again, fellow travelers came to our rescue, sharing their photos of Galapagos' wonderful works of nature.

Upon our return to the United States, we were pleasantly surprised to find the manufacturer of the camera was willing to back it up, even though it had been purchased in Bolivia. In a matter of a few weeks, it was returned to us, fully operational.

We still have it, and over the years, it has taken many beautiful photographs of our exploits of Southeast Asia, China, Korea as well as a host of family pictures.

CHAPTER 21

The Best Snorkeling

We find snorkeling to be immensely enjoyable and an inexpensive traveler's sport. A simple mask and air tube enable one to appreciate the gentle waters and colorful fish and coral around the world. The equipment is lightweight and easy to transport in a backpack. We stopped using fins years ago, as they are big and clumsy to pack and don't add much to the experience.

Our current set of snorkel equipment was purchased used, in the back-packer area of Bangkok. They cost a mere four dollars and serve as excellent gear. Having them with us when we travel enables us to take advantage of any snorkeling opportunity that presents itself.

Another hobby we casually indulge in while traveling is bird watching. A small bird book for reference and a pair of binoculars are the only requirements. We always carry binoculars with us anyway, to view natural wonders, so the addition of a bird book is minor. The unexpected sighting of a Bali Starling in the wild brings joy to the heart.

Although not butterfly enthusiasts, we will never forget the moment we saw a Rajah Brooke's Birdwing butterfly in the wilds of Borneo. It is an unforgettable experience that we have fondly looked back upon innumerable times, reflecting upon its brilliance.

In addition to viewing these various works of nature, they also serve as subjects for my amateurish hobby of oil painting. All of these simple pleasures are there for our contemplation at low cost and with little effort.

On our travels, we have frequently been asked *Where is the best snorkeling?* We have tried many of the more famous and lesser-known locations. The Pacific coast of Mexico, the reef off Belize, and the Yucatan coast, as well as the islands of Cozumel and Isla Mujeres have all provided extraordinary entertainment. We have also taken expeditions in the Caribbean Islands and spent time snorkeling around the Galapagos Islands, all of which were beautiful. In the east, we have enjoyed snorkeling coral reefs off both Thai and Indonesian Islands. The island of Fiji has also provided great delights.

With all these places in mind, we answer the question of the best snorkeling in a two-fold manner. When we snorkel, we admire both the fish and the coral. Some locations have the most fascinating and brilliant fish to view while others feature elegant corals with a limited variety of fish.

Much of the world's coral has been destroyed by man, so we often encounter colorful fish with the encircling damaged coral. The current efforts to save coral reefs should be applauded and supported, for at the current rate of destruction, little will be left for future generations to enjoy.

With regard to coral, we have found the Great Barrier Reef off the northeast coast of Australia to be without equal. We had occasion to snorkel Kelsey Reef, which encompasses a small portion of the Great Reef. The coral there has a spectacular array of colors and shapes and made for a truly magical experience. Kelsey Reef has a gleaming array of aquatic life, but it was the beauty of the coral reef that we found most fascinating. The blazing sun on that particular day added to the spectacle of colors. Oranges, blues, greens, yellows, and reds were optimum as we spent hours at sea, thoroughly enjoying nature's serenade. It is little wonder that the Great Barrier Reef has been the subject of so many television documentaries. However, television cameras can never convey the joy in snorkeling this marvel.

With regard to viewing the most amazing display of fish, our story goes back to when we met Tim at a beach in southern Mexico. He had spent years as a master diver in the United States Navy and had a full array of sea stories to tell, as he had spent over three decades diving and snorkeling around the world.

After chatting off and on for three days while resting in our hammocks under a palapa, I asked him the big question: Where is the best snorkeling?

To which he answered, "You may not have heard of this place, but there is a small island off the northwest coast of Bali called Menjangen and it has amazing snorkeling."

"How do we find it? I wondered aloud.

"It's about fifty kilometers due west of the Bali resort area called Lovina. Just catch a bus from Lovina to the national park, then catch a boat to get to Menjangen," he answered.

Although I did not have pen and paper in hand, I recorded the information in my mind in the event we ever went to Indonesia. Low and behold, the very next year, Christine and I were traveling on the north coast of Bali.

Having read about the area in our guidebook, we realized the potential of encountering many tourists snorkeling the reef. Planning ahead, we made arrangements with a Dutch couple to arrive bright and early one morning. Sharing the boat with the other twosome, we were the only four people snorkeling the reef for the first several hours.

The boat excursion from Bali to Menjangen took about thirty minutes. Depositing us on a small beach, the boatman directed us to the reef a mere fifty feet off shore. What we observed was the most dazzling display of sea creatures that we have ever encountered.

The island and reef are a protected area so people are encouraged not to feed the fish or damage the reef. The area was entirely intact and in its own natural state.

With the bright sun illuminating the objects of our quest to true brilliance, we were in for an eye-awakening experience. The fish were of all colors and sizes and were totally unfazed by our presence as we meandered through the various schools. Words or photographs could never adequately describe the sight.

Thanks to Tim, we are able to answer part two of the question: Where is the best snorkeling? Menjangen Island was where we found the most dazzling display of fish we have ever encountered.

One need not travel to Australia or Indonesia to enjoy good snorkeling. Caribbean Islands and the coast of Mexico have provided us with hours of glorious underwater exploration. Many travelers have expounded on the wonders of the Red Sea. We cannot comment on that area, as we have not seen that part of the world, yet.

CHAPTER 22

The Energy of Machu Picchu

Machu Picchu was an archeological site Christine and I had wanted to see most of our lives. Only having been discovered by the western world in 1911, it had a mystical appeal to both of us. We wondered why any civilization would have established a city in such a remote place.

The train ride from Cusco to Aguas Calientes is by far the most spectacular we have ever taken. The snow-capped peaks to our right with the backdrop of a clear blue sky was truly breathtaking. Two years prior, we rode the rail through the Copper Canyon of Mexico, which we thought was the ultimate train ride, but the beauty of the high Andes was far superior in radiance and splendor. The colorful Peruvian Indians selling their goods added to the fascination. It was beyond what we had anticipated.

Aguas Calientes is a small tourist town at the base of the mountain upon which Machu Picchu is set. It is named after the hot springs that come out of the ground nearby. It served as our base from which we visited the archeological site.

Upon arrival in the town, we quickly found ourselves a guesthouse among many to choose from, then took the next bus up the mountain. Although we planned to stay in Aguas Calientes for several days and had plenty of time to see Machu

Picchu, we felt an eagerness, like children wanting to open their gifts on Christmas morning.

The road up the mountain had a multitude of hairpin curves. It took us nearly half an hour to traverse the short distance. We reached the site in all its splendor at approximately two in the afternoon, which gave us several hours of exploratory time before returning to our lodging. With a map of the ancient metropolis in hand, we ventured through the old stone foundations one by one. The locations of the various temples were always of interest, for they usually stand high above other sites, offering the most magnificent views. The panorama of the rugged Andes was imposing at sunset with its mystical clouds engulfing the immediate summit.

In three hours, we had managed a quick look over the old city. We decided on an early rise the next morning, which would enable us to catch the first vehicle heading up the mountain. We wanted to beat the crowd of tourists that normally arrive around eleven o'clock. We longed to have the place to ourselves for as long as possible during the early morning hours. We also wanted to watch the sunrise from the top of the ridge.

With picnic in hand, we boarded the bus at 6:30 the next morning and ventured up the mountain for a second time. Much to our liking, we found that we were two of only a half dozen travelers at this early hour. With the massive area Machu Picchu encompasses, it basically meant that we had the place to ourselves for the next several hours. As expected, we did not encounter any of the other travelers during the early part of the day.

There is nothing like experiencing Machu Picchu firsthand. The sanctuary sits in a large saddle between two mountain peaks. Its size and location are impressive, as was the sunrise that day. The sun seemed to make its presence slowly, in the mist of the mountains. It was a glorious, gradual illumination.

Our goal for the day was to explore a variety of locations we had glossed over the previous day, and to devote ample time to the sites of most interest. First on our list was the Temple of the Sun.

"It's over this way," I said, pointing to my left.

She was observing the stonework of an arched entrance. "I'll be right with you."

Within moments, we were standing on a huge boulder overlooking the remains of the circular shaped Temple of the Sun.

After circumventing the religious site, Christine said, "I'd like to have a look at it from down below, as well as a second glimpse of the cave we saw yesterday."

Walking around via a convoluted pathway, we eventually reached the underside where the small cave is located. This time around, we sat near the entrance of the cave, admiring the marvelous surrounding stonework which supports the temple. The Incas were excellent stonemasons and their handy work was enthralling.

While preparing for a photograph, Christine looked at me and asked, "Do you feel that?"

I looked at her hesitatingly, "Do you mean that force coming from the cave?"

"Yes, feel it?" she asked again, "I wonder what it is."

It felt like an unimaginable field of energy, coming from beneath the temple. It was not magnetism, gravity, or suction. It felt like being enclosed in a warm, comforting cloud of strength and well-being. No experience in our lives could explain it, but the force was certainly there. Needless to say, we remained fixed to the location for some time. We contemplated the likelihood that ancient Incas established their city on this saddle between the two peaks because of the force. They must have known it was there to have erected the temple immediately above the source of energy. It must have felt like a magical place to them, as it had for the two of us.

"What did they know about energy and forces that has long been forgotten?" I wondered aloud. The only things that remain from many ancient civilizations are stonework, metalwork, ceramics, and the like, but what about their knowledge? How much did the Mayan priests or Incas know that has been devoured in the course of human civilization?

"This force *has* to be the reason for the existence of this city. It is so remote from the remainder of the empire. And so difficult to reach," Christine said.

After about thirty minutes of observation and discussion, we decided to move on for a better look at the irrigation and drainage system that were very much in operation in this moist atmosphere.

After a couple of hours meandering about, my wife suggested we return to the Temple of the Sun. In particular, she wanted to go back to the cave. Our experience with the force marveled us. "It is such a special place," she said.

Once again, we felt the force as we stood in awe of what we were experiencing.

By now, tour groups were beginning to arrive and a very curious thing happened. A group of approximately ten tourists and their English-speaking Peruvian guide came to the area where we were standing. We listened as he explained the intricacies of the stonework that went into building the cave which served as the temple's foundation.

In the course of the guide's explanations, an Australian member of the group stepped up and with his hands forward of his body, he openly interjected, "Can you feel that?"

There was no response from the group, so he further questioned, "Do you feel the energy?"

Still, there were no remarks from his travel companions. He looked around and asked again, "Don't you feel it?"

Brushing the Australian's vocal interlude aside, the tour guide directed the group to move on to the next site and then began to lead the assembly of people away.

Christine and I looked at each other.

"It's real," she proclaimed.

"You're right. It's not only us."

The Australian fellow had supported our claim without knowing it. I still berate myself for not speaking up to defend him. Although they dismissed him, we knew exactly what he was talking about.

To this day, Christine and I discuss the forces of the universe that we expect are there, but cannot feel, see, or comprehend. We always show respect and appreciation for shamans or Indian groups that appear to be energized by invisible forces. Just because we do not feel what they feel, does not mean that it doesn't exist. To discount ancient civilizations' knowledge of things beyond our comprehension may be shortchanging their understanding of the universe.

We spent the remainder of the day exploring the nooks and crannies of Machu Picchu, but none of our experiences that day would rival the force beneath the Temple of the Sun. It was an inexplicable dream come true, an unforgettable epiphany.

CHAPTER 23

Pishing for Birds

Could we afford a side trip to the Galapagos Islands, off the coast of Ecuador? That was the question confronting us as we bused north of Lima. We had read and been told by many travelers not to book Galapagos trips until you arrive in Quito. Then book passage onto a boat at the last minute, in effort to get the best price.

We were waiting, as we could not afford to do otherwise. We concluded that if we could get a good price, we would take on the expedition. All that we had read and seen on documentary films indicated that it was a special place to observe birds and animals, an experience we would treasure.

Upon arrival in Ecuador's capital, we found the tales fellow travelers had shared to be true. There were indeed great deals to be found if one shopped around from one travel agency to another.

Research at the South American Explorers Club, of which we were members, provided us with detailed information to make knowledgeable decisions regarding our proposed venture. We were directed to an agency that had last minute offers including arranged flights to and from the Islands at preset prices, along with a venture on a large ship that would be exploring the Islands for seven days. This worked for us, as the seven days as well as the faster speed of the larger vessel would enable us to see some of the more distant islands.

After booking our boat and flight, we quickly packed one backpack, leaving most of our luggage behind at the Explorers Club. Our plane was leaving the next morning for the Islands.

Christine and I rarely travel on package tours. However, for this trip, it made sense and really made life effortless. We were met at the airport by the ship's staff and bused directly to the dock where we immediately embarked on our ship. Within two hours of our flight's arrival, we were on our way to viewing our first Galapagos seals and Darwin finches while trekking over massive lava fields.

Our group of ten people was named "Cormorants" and led by a most able guide named Raymundo. Only official guides approved by the government office are allowed to lead groups. We soon learned that not all guides are of equal caliber. Lucky for us, Raymundo was outstanding. So much so, that other travelers on our ship, though members of other groups, slipped over to join our group.

"One of these days, we will go pishing," Raymundo told us on our second day, while we observed a flock of nesting blue-footed boobies.

"What's this pishing?" I asked the British couple that joined our table for lunch.

They had no idea but were equally intrigued.

Meals on board the ship were especially enjoyable. The food was excellent, but more important and interesting, were the people from various places around the world. Conversations of people's lives and experiences were interspersed with talk about flightless cormorants and

Galapagos penguins. It was an exhilarating mix of people and adventure.

Raymundo also became a topic of discussion with his intricate knowledge of the mating rituals of seafaring iguanas versus land iguanas. His demonstrations of the various courting habits led to much laughter. His understanding of the varying behavior patterns of birds and animals from one island to another was simply astonishing.

Finally, one morning, our enthusiastic guide said, "Okay, today we are going pishing."

Once again, I asked an anticipating traveler if he knew what pishing was.

"Who knows?" he responded, and went on to say that he had asked around the ship but nobody seemed to know.

By now, we had faith in Raymundo and were prepared to follow him on his pishing expedition. Finally, while on the trail of giant land turtles on Elizabeth Island, he stopped near a desolate bush and stated, "Now is the time for pishing."

As we watched in dazzling amazement, Raymundo extended his arm toward the barren bush, devoid of any animals or birds and began to whisper, "Pish, Pish, Pish." Nothing happened, but he continued, "Pish, Pish, Pish." All the time, he kept his arm stretched outward.

After a couple of minutes of this "Pish, Pish, Pish," birds began to fly into the bush. The more he called them, the closer they came to him. They hopped from limb to limb until they finally reached his extended hand.

Over the next several days, Raymundo was able to demonstrate his ability to call birds to him on more than one occasion. His pishing worked every time. The birds seemed to come out of nowhere, attracted by his call.

To this day, we do not know if pishing is unique to Raymundo, but can attest to his incredible ability to summon the creatures at his discretion.

Raymundo had an intricate knowledge of the birds, animals, and aquatic life that inhabit these marvelous islands. We were not surprised to hear that he would be featured on a documentary about the Galapagos Islands. His reputation extended well beyond our group and we were fortunate to have his commentaries.

As for the Islands, we found them to be a land of wonders. In a world where most animals have learned to fear man, this archipelago was a place where man and animals could cohabit in a friendly manner. The isolation of the Islands had not only encouraged the development of unique species, but also allowed distinctive forms of behavior that one does not readily see in other parts of the world.

We will always hold dear our venture to the Galapagos Islands, where we enjoyed behaving like tourists while viewing and learning about this very unique habitat.

CHAPTER 24

Five Weeks in Patzcuaro

We were on a seven-month journey through Mexico with our van. After having spent twelve days in Taxco enjoying the festivities of *Semana Santa* (Easter Week), we were moving on to Patzcuaro. Two years prior, we had spent four days there and were eager to spend another four days in this high-altitude city.

Being one of the most prominent handicraft areas in Mexico, Christine was looking forward to not only visiting the town itself, but also browsing through several adjoining villages. We arrived late on a Wednesday and immediately located sleeping quarters that were comfortable and relatively inexpensive at twelve dollars per night.

The following morning, as we walked towards Once Patios, the large craft area, my lovely wife suggested that we try and get to Paracho, where they hand-make guitars.

I was in favor of the idea and recalled reading about a guitar festival that would take place in Paracho later in the month.

"I read about it too," Christine said, "but I think we'll be in Oaxaca by then."

"Okay, maybe next time."

"Tomorrow, we should drive out to Santa Clara del Cobre," she chatted on. "It's only ten kilometers from here.

They're reputed to have the best hand-made copperware in Mexico."

"I'd love to go there," I said enthusiastically.

Stopping for a morning coffee, Christine also mentioned that we should get out to Tzintzuntzan.

"How far is that?" I asked.

"Not far at all, and there's a lot to see there according to the book," she responded.

"What is that place known for?"

"They make very pretty ceramics and have a famous archeological site. It would be an all-day expedition," she added.

"Sounds like an interesting place," I remarked, as the list went on.

"This whole area abounds in arts and crafts. That's what it's known for," she stated.

I then facetiously said, "Maybe we ought to rent a house and stay a while."

To that, she stated, "I read about a guy in *AIM* Magazine, named Robert Jones, who rents out houses and apartments in Patzcuaro."

I chuckled at her immediate reference. Within a minute or two, I realized she also had the landlord's phone number so we could reach him if we so desired.

At this stage of the conversation, there was no question in my mind that Christine had an appetite for Patzcuaro and its environs. Our short stay two years ago, along with having read books on Mexican crafts, had developed her interest in seeing the area thoroughly.

I submitted readily, knowing she had her heart set on the place. We had plenty of time on our hands and I really liked the town.

"I'll give a call to that fellow with the houses for rent after we return from Once Patios," I responded, and for which I received a big kiss.

As promised, later that day, I called Robert. After looking at several of his properties, Christine and I ended up renting a furnished house for a month. The month became five weeks, as we ended up extending our rental period. As difficult as it may be to believe, we had not visited all the places we wanted to see by the end of our original four-week time period.

The weeks went by fast. As well as observing woodcarvers, coppersmiths, weavers, and artists at work, we visited furniture makers, orchards, markets, and a series of ancient archeological sites, not to mention two festivals which abounded in music, fireworks, food, and drink.

To compliment all of these enjoyable activities, we took two weeks of Spanish lessons in effort to enhance our ability to communicate with Mexicans. Taking classes in the morning enabled us to continue our quest for handcrafts during the afternoons.

Patzcuaro is a lovely little city that sits on the banks of a large lake called Lago Patzcuaro. Many little villages are found on the road surrounding the mass of water, which makes for a picturesque drive.

The house we rented sat on a hill overlooking the lake. A huge deck on the second level had us lazing around in our hammocks in the evenings. On chilly nights, we lit the fireplace and indulged in some home cooking, which is a rarity when traveling.

Continually in search of a place to settle when we retire, we gave Patzcuaro serious consideration. It is very authentic with few gringo tourists, which is very appealing. Many Mexicans visit on weekends from the capital, but other than that, it is very quiet. The relatively small size of the community precludes an abundance of cultural activities but the larger city of Morelia is only about fifty kilometers away. The only real negative, in our opinion, is the cool temperature brought on by the elevation of over six thousand feet.

Though we abandoned thoughts of settling there on a permanent basis, we must confess to having thoroughly enjoyed our five-week stay. Our Spanish improved, which was critical for our future travels in Central and South America, and we experienced many of Mexico's lovely people and handcrafts firsthand.

The travel lesson from our Patzcuaro experience is to remain as flexible and open as possible. When we find a place that we truly take pleasure in, we try to stick around to take in the sights and people. Some places, be they small towns, cities, natural wonders, or archeological sites take extra time to fully appreciate.

Five weeks in Patzcuaro was none too long. We were happy to be able to extend our stay and hope to return someday for a third visit.

CHAPTER 25

Dengue Fever

We had allocated two weeks of rest and relaxation at a beach in Ecuador, after having spent the last nine months in Central America, Peru, Bolivia, and the Galapagos Islands. We just had to figure out which beach would be best for us. None of the *playas* listed in the guidebook sounded like what we were looking for.

Our initial plan was to fly back to Quito from the Galapagos, stay a few days, then bus to the coastal area of our choice.

"I'd hate to go all the way there and not like it though," Christine mentioned.

That had happened to us before—a long, jolting ride that was totally unrewarding.

"Nothing is guaranteed. It'll be hit or miss until we find what we like," I said, when a flicker of an idea came to mind.

"Why an Ecuadorian beach?" I asked. "Here's an alternative idea. Let's fly from Quito to Guatemala tomorrow, then bus to San Agustinillo in Southern Mexico."

The issue was the ride from Guatemala City to the beach in Southern Mexico. It would take twenty-four hours, but at the end of the voyage, we knew we would be in a beautiful setting. By consolidating our transportation schedule in this manner, we calculated we could spend twenty-eight days at the beach, then bus up to Mexico City, from where we could fly to the United States. Although it would mean a difficult two days of travel up front, we decided to embark on this new schedule.

The plan worked well. We arrived at San Agustinillo and were able to relax under a palapa and catch up on rest. The sea breeze and ocean waters felt wonderful.

Christine and I are always particular about getting the necessary travel shots as well as taking preventive medications for malaria. Over the years, we have witnessed firsthand the effects of hepatitis, malaria, and had heard of people getting dengue fever. There is no preventive medication or shot for dengue, so all you can do is try to prevent mosquito bites and hope you don't get it.

San Agustinillo had mosquitoes, but by taking our malaria medication, we had never had a problem.

Our first twenty days at the beach were as uneventful as we had anticipated and hoped for. A mix of reading, bird watching, swimming, and walking was the perfect antidote for our previous nine months of travel. The twenty-eight days would have been perfect, except that on the twenty-second day, Christine woke up with a fever and severe headache. The fever must have been at least 103, though we did not have a thermometer. As the day wore on, she began to ache all over.

On the second day, I decided to search out an American nurse that we knew was staying at the beach. Jane and her friend Susan, the nurse, came over. Susan thought it could be meningitis. Dengue fever did not enter her mind, as she was not familiar with tropical diseases.

Jane, who lived at the beach as a permanent resident, volunteered to drive us to a medical doctor the next day, if the fever did not diminish.

Much to our dismay, Christine's temperature did not let up, and the next morning, Jane took us to see Dr. Renardo. He was a Mexican doctor who generously gave most of his time to an orphanage of infirmed children. He was always there for those in need, and fortunately, he was able to see Christine immediately.

As he took her temperature, he asked how long she had been at the beach.

"We've been here three weeks."

One hundred four degrees." He then asked, "How does your body feel?"

"It aches all over."

"It's dengue fever," he stated. "The incubation period is twenty-one days from the time a mosquito bites."

"What can you do for her?" I asked.

"There is no cure, but she can take five hundred milligrams of Tylenol to assist in alleviating the aches and fever. However, be certain not to take aspirin," he directed. "Dengue can, in rare instances, cause internal bleeding and aspirin can complicate things," he responded.

"How long will this last?" Christine asked.

"Only a few more days," he said, then generously offered his services in the future, if need be.

Jane was good enough to drive us to a pharmacy thirty kilometers away, and Christine went on her regimen of Tylenol while suffering miserably the next several days.

Upon further reading, we learned that dengue fever is a tropical disease introduced to the body by a mosquito during daytime. It is often called "breakbone" fever because the patient feels like all of his or her bones are being squeezed along with the aches accompanying the fever.

We later concluded that it was better that Christine developed the symptoms in Mexico rather than after returning to the States. Dr Renardo was much more familiar with the disease than most western doctors and could accurately diagnose within five minutes. It may have taken a physician in the United States much more time along with many tests to reach the same diagnoses.

Dengue has no long-term effect, as malaria sometimes does, so Christine was free and clear of the disease within a few days.

As planned, we left for Mexico City on the twenty-eighth day, although it took another month for her to fully regain her strength. Like a true warrior, she did not let dengue diminish her interest and desire for travel. After two months in the United States, we were on the road again, venturing to Southeast Asia.

CHAPTER 26

Ninety-Three and Still Traveling

The majority of travelers we encounter are from Germany, France, and England, less from Australia and other parts of the world. We meet very few from the United States as we ply the environs of the world. Most Americans seem to tour the United States and its immediate neighbors rather than travel afar. Many Europeans, of course, have the decided advantage of six-week vacations each year.

Travelers, by and large, are in their early to mid-twenties, not having embarked on a career yet. However, we do seem to meet more and more middle-aged people on the road.

We were in Oaxaca, Mexico, this particular July and were planning to attend the Fourth of July celebration dinner being sponsored by the English language subscription library. It is always enjoyable to hear Americans tell their tales of adventure, living in a foreign environment.

We arrived early at Llano Park to meet the private bus that would transport us to the restaurant and festivities. While waiting, we began conversing with an elderly gentleman who was waiting for his wife.

"We're only in Oaxaca for six weeks this time, but we've been here many times before," he stated. "We were here for six months three years ago."

"You must like it," I commented.

"We do. The people are lovely and we enjoy the climate."

As the bus arrived, he excused himself and quickly trotted off in search of his wife who had gone to the pharmacy.

Once on the coach, Christine and I talked with other American devotees. Upon arrival at the party, we made our way through the crowd during the cocktail hour, enjoying the chitchat. With the sound of the bell, we proceeded to the magnificent buffet dinner and found seats at a vacant table.

Three other couples soon joined us at our table for eight. As we all introduced ourselves, I noticed the couple sitting across from us was the elderly man we had met at the park, along with his wife.

We enjoyed our meal and conversation continued with small tidbits of information from him and his wife. They told us that they were first here in '55, that they were in China with one of the first groups, and that they were somewhere else before World War II. They also mentioned travels in Indonesia, New Zealand, and Russia.

As the conversation continued, it became clear that they had been traveling the world decades before we had ever imagined such a thing. It made me wonder, just how old were they? I wanted to inquire, but in effort to mind my manners, I asked instead, "How long have you been traveling this year?".

"Only six weeks. As I mentioned earlier, I had open-heart surgery last summer and Sally had a stroke two years ago, so we don't travel nearly as much as we would like."

"Sorry to hear that," Christine said.

My curiosity got the better of me. I finally asked, "How old are you folks?"

Not the least bit embarrassed, the gentleman proudly answered, "I'm ninety-three and Sally is ninety-one."

I was amazed and stunned. Not only did they not look their ages, but he had literally *trotted off* to look for his wife at the park earlier. They visited Oaxaca for six weeks—in their nineties. Most Americans would not make that same trip to southern Mexico during their twenties, much less in late retirement.

As conversations proceeded and we began to talk about our proposed trip to Asia the following year, I was dazzled to discover that they were entertaining a trip to Australia. "Only for a month," Sally said, giggling.

When optimistically discussing our future, Christine and I often refer to our Fourth of July celebration with the traveling ninety-year-olds. "If only we could be that energetic and still be traveling at ninety-three," I often remark.

We bid farewell to the lovely couple after dinner, never to see them again, though we thoroughly enjoyed our chance meeting.

Since that time, we have also met a ninety-one-year-old traveler from Lakeville, Massachusetts. At last encounter, she had spent several weeks in Italy visiting Rome and was planning a Mississippi River excursion on the Delta Queen. Her eyes lit up as we described *Semana Santa* in Mexico, which she added to her list of places to go.

We cannot all be as fortunate as these elder travelers, but it is always inspiring to see people energetically accepting new challenges during their later stages of life.

CHAPTER 27

A Nail in the Door

We had found our way to the coastal town of Zihuatenejo on our seven-month tour of Mexico. We were looking for a beach to relax for a week before heading south to Acapulco and then on to Taxco, the famous silver mining town. It was near the end of our journey and we were a bit weary, in need of a break.

Zihua, as the locals call it, is part fishing village, part small tourist city. The quaintness of the place disappeared when the large modern resort of Ixtapa, with its multi-story hotels, was developed only ten kilometers away. Neither of the two locations were what we were seeking. Ixtapa was too expensive and modern, and Zihua was more city-like than we wanted. Although the town has a beach, it was not the quiet, slow-paced type of atmosphere we were looking for at this stage of our trip.

"I saw a small write-up in the guidebook about a place called Barra de Potosi," Christine mentioned as we strolled the beach. "It's only about twenty kilometers south."

"What does the book say about it?"

"Not much, just that it has a thirty-kilometer beach and it's mostly uninhabited."

"The place sounds perfect to me. Let's go to the tourist office to get some directions and information," I suggested.

At the Zihuatenejo tourist office, they gave us simple directions: Drive south for ten kilometers to a small village, then turn right. Drive another ten kilometers on a very rough road, and you will come to the beach."

"Are there any directional signs?" I asked.

"Sorry sir, it's not a very popular place," the woman responded.

"Are there any hotels?" Christine asked in her rough, but rapidly improving Spanish.

"Maybe a guesthouse or two. I don't really know."

The next morning, we were on our way, bright and early, to find Barra de Potosi. It was straightforward enough, but the road was a disaster. To say that it was rough was putting it mildly. In one area, our old van had to make its way through a river. The last half of the drive took nearly an hour, but the magnificent beach made it worth the effort.

The beach was thirty kilometers long, as Christine had read, with beautiful rolling waves. At one end was a jutting peninsula with a mountain, ready for climbing. On the back of the peninsula, a lagoon, perfect for exploring by canoe. To add to the appeal, Christine and I were the only tourists there. In fact, there was hardly anybody around.

"How about stopping at one of those little fish restaurants and having a coffee? Christine suggested. "At the same time, we can ask about lodging."

"Sounds good." As I drove slowly around the multitude of potholes, I noticed and pointed out a large shell of a building.

"Looks like somebody is working on it," my wife said.

"Someday it could be a nice place. It certainly is big enough, and it's right on the beach."

We stopped at a small fishing village with a row of approximately ten restaurants. As far as we could observe, they all had very similar menus. We settled at the fourth, no-name establishment, enjoyed a cup of coffee, and inquired about lodging. In response, the waitress pointed to the rundown one-story building to the rear of the restaurant.

"It doesn't look promising," I said to Christine.

"No, it does not, but let's have a look anyway."

After the coffee, a quick look at the guesthouse confirmed our original assumption—musty and dirty, no good.

Driving back along the beach, I said, "Let's stop by the big place that's under construction. At least it's on the beach, and who knows, maybe they'll have something."

The future two-story, motel-style building looked as though it would someday have twenty or so rooms. Although the structure was merely a frame, it appeared that two of the downstairs rooms were enclosed.

Walking toward the building, we heard noise coming from one of the enclosed areas.

"Let's see who's there," I suggested.

Upon entering, we saw a middle-aged Mexican man painting the ceiling. Except for the ladder and paint can, the voluminous room was empty. A look through the spacious window transfixed our eyes on a picturesque view of the ocean with its magnificent sound reverberating in our ears.

"*Tienes un cuarto?*" I asked in Spanish. Do you have a room?

It became clear from his response that he was the owner and no, he did not have an available room.

"*Gracias,*" I thanked him as we turned to leave.

Walking out, we heard him say, "*A la mañana.*" This is the famous Mexican phrase for tomorrow.

We turned to face him and simultaneously repeated, "*Mañana?*"

With a smile on his face, he pointed to the floor and said, "*Aqui,*" which means here.

"*Y un cama?*" I asked, pointing to where the bed should be.

"*Si, si,*" he added.

Without hesitation, we stepped forward to shake his hand and confirmed we would be here by eleven the following morning.

All we talked about was the view and the roar of the ocean at dinner that evening, though we were a bit concerned about the preparedness of the room. In Mexico, one day often leads to the next, and nothing much seems to get done. We would soon find out, as we intended to be there at eleven the next morning, luggage in hand.

Jose and his wife Emelia greeted us as we drove up the following morning. Hugging and shaking hands, they escorted us to our room. It seemed a bit ceremonious, but we were the first to rent a room. The building was projected to be a twenty-room hotel. It was their dream come true, although it clearly had a long way to go.

Upon entering the room, we realized Jose had lived up to his word and more. Not only was there a bed, there was also a chair next to the bed. The bed and chair seemed lost in the immensity of the room, but at least we had a peaceful place to settle for the week.

As we began to unpack our things, Christine mentioned that it would be nice to have a place to hang things.

On our way to the beach for a swim, I saw Jose and mentioned Christine's request.

"No problem," he answered in English.

We thanked him as we made our way to the makeshift palapa on the beach. Although crude, the palapa provided the shade to make our stay comfortable. After an hour of swimming and relaxing in our hammocks, we returned to the room.

Once again, Jose was there with his perpetual grin and led us to our room. Upon entering, he closed the door and pointed to a nail he had hammered in on the inside of the door.

It was clear from the appearance on his face that he was proud of his solution to our problem. In his mind, we had a place to hang our clothes.

Being aware of the sensitivity of the moment, we smiled and thanked him.

After his departure, we looked at each other and chuckled, understanding we would have to live with a bed, a chair, and a nail in the door. A photograph of a shirt hanging from the lone nail now immortalizes our photo album for that year.

We stayed there for one wonderful week. Walks on the beach, excellent seafood, a climb up the mountain, and making our way through the lagoon in a dugout canoe are but a few of the activities that complemented our reading in hammocks under Jose's palapa.

We have since returned to *Posada Potosi*, as Jose and Emelia later named their hotel. They now have fifteen rooms completed and many improvements. Jose and Emilia have a grand design with a magnificent location, but their interior design skills are limited. After seven years, we have yet to see a room adorned with a picture on the wall, though he has replaced the nail in the door with a wooden clothes rack and wire hangers.

We will likely return again to *Posada Potosi*, as we find the combination of friendly hosts and a beautiful beach to be superb. It is undoubtedly a great place to unwind and let time pass.

CHAPTER 28

The Ring that Changed Color

Cusco, Peru is one of those cities that people come to visit for a week, but end up staying the next twenty years. In our brief one-week visit, we encountered a host of North Americans and Europeans who had extended their sojourn for years on end, opening a little business or teaching English as a means of sustenance.

Although too cold for our blood, it is easy to see how the ambiance of the city and its geographical setting entice people into remaining. The old metropolis, built of stone by the Incas, Spanish, and Peruvians, has an air of antiquity that can easily lead to one falling in love with the place instantly. The surrounding Andes Mountains provide spectacular panoramic views in all directions. A short pilgrimage out of town offers the exploration of multiple Incan ruins while pleasantly hiking the mountainous trails.

Christine and I are not hikers, yet we could not turn our back on such adventure. We bused away from Cusco for one hour, into the higher altitudes of the mountains. Returning to town on foot through the hilly terrain enabled us to visit one archeological site after another while taking in the scenic beauty of the Andes. The intense terracing throughout the area displayed the strenuous agricultural pursuits of the

Indian forbearers. An ice-cold beer in a backwater Indian village was a perfect break in the midst of the challenging day.

We were not only in Cusco to take in the scenery and sites of the area, but also to purchase the perfect silver ring, with a dark, striped malachite setting. Of the many gift items sold in this town, silver jewelry is by far the most popular. It seemed that every other store was a jewelry establishment. There are probably fifty stores specializing in the precious metal. The tradition of silverwork dates back over five hundred years and we found a multitude of what appeared to be quality work.

After asking around for suggestions at the South American Explorers Club and at our convent/hotel, we set out in earnest to find that perfect ring. Two days later, after looking at and trying on hundreds of specimens, we found one that I loved. It was rounded for a snug fit on my right-hand ring finger, with three deep green, striped stones crossing the center at a slight angle. After some difficult negotiations, I proudly wore my newly acquired possession as we visited old cathedrals and museums.

With our week rapidly coming to an end, Christine suggested we bus to the hot springs twenty-kilometers from the city.

"An excellent idea," I concurred.

The next morning, with bathing suits and towels in hand, we caught an early ride to the enticing springs.

Although not too far away, we felt like we really needed the hot bath by the time we arrived. The dusty road was laden with so many potholes and switchbacks that we wished we had taken motion sickness medication.

An hour and a half after our departure, we arrived at the village with the hot springs and enjoyed the next several hours in the luxury and comfort that nature provided. Being a weekday, there were few locals around and only two other travelers. It was a perfect setting, deep within a river valley, surrounded by lush greenery, and with songbirds in abundance.

Stepping out from the water, we began walking down the ravine toward the shower and changing rooms, before catching a vehicle back to Cusco.

"It sure was relaxing," I mentioned to Christine while I happened to glance down at my ring. To my amazement, it had changed color, from silver to an off-yellow. Before Christine could react to what I had said, I interjected, "Look at this!" directing her observation to my finger.

She must have sensed that my blood pressure had risen as I exclaimed in disappointment, "Would you believe it?"

"We can return it and get our money back as soon as we get into town," she suggested. Further trying to appease me, she volunteered, "We'll find another. There are plenty to choose from."

I was completely deflated by the experience, questioning the value of Peruvian silver.

We went in for showers, and being the first one done, I entered the cafeteria for a Coke. While sipping, I began to rub my ring with the towel. To my surprise, the yellow coloring immediately came off and the silver luster reappeared. It was like magic. I was as pleased as punch.

As Christine returned from her shower, I said, "Look here, pointing to the ring with a big smile on my face."

"What happened?" she asked.

"I just wiped it off with my towel, and it's like new."

"We can still return it, if you'd like," she offered.

"No, I love this one. This is the one I'd like to keep."

We concluded that mineral elements in the hot spring must have caused a chemical reaction, which discolored the silver. A gentle wiping cleared it up and it has remained as it should ever since, even after extensive wearing over the past several years.

Though I shall always remember Cusco for its antiquarian beauty, I will also always recall, and laugh a little, at my brief upset followed by relief concerning my perfect silver malachite ring.

CHAPTER 29

Popcorn and Potatoes

Bolivia was a land with many surprises for us, but nothing we had read prepared us for the huge array of potatoes.

"Did you notice all the potatoes in the market?" I asked Christine.

"They were all over the place!"

"I have never seen so many different kinds in all my life," I exclaimed.

"There must have been at least twenty varieties," she commented.

Later that evening, we read that not only were potatoes the staple crop of the nation, but some people claimed there were up to six hundred various types that were grown in this land of high elevation. We never saw *that* many different kinds in any one market, but the largest selection was at the Cochabamba market. An expansive portion of the mercado was devoted exclusively to potatoes.

While browsing the market area, Christine had an idea. "Let's have a potato tasting."

"A what?"

"You've been to wine tastings and clam chowder tastings, why not a potato tasting?"

"Yes, that's true enough. And they *have* been enjoyable, but where do you plan to cook this medley?" I questioned.

"Simple," she responded. "I'll ask the owner of the guesthouse to use her kitchen, and we can do it at lunch tomorrow."

I should have realized that she had it all planned out in her head. That evening, the owner of our residence gave us a cook's tour of her kitchen and willingly gave Christine permission to utilize the facility the next day.

Cochabamba, although in the heart of the Andes, sits in a low fertile valley. The weather is very mild in spite of being surrounded by high mountain peaks. The city of three hundred thousand inhabitants can be enjoyed in shirtsleeves with its mostly sunny skies. This particular day was typical as we meandered several kilometers to the marketplace.

We had decided the previous evening that our tasting should only include ten different types of potatoes. We also agreed to limit our purchases to two specimens of each. Even that would involve a whole lot of eating.

The vendors looked at us questioningly, as we prodded through, selecting a couple from this basket and a couple from that pile. We had no guidance in this venture, so we just selected what looked appealing.

That noon, we had a feast that was delightful to the palate. Adorned with local herbs, we tasted each variety, one by one, and found they each had distinct flavors and textures. Some were spicy, others sweet like yams. Some were crisp as apples, even when cooked, others floury. The colors ranged from usual shades of white and yellow through to purple and an unappetizing black. Christine's idea had made for an interesting afternoon.

Whenever we are in foreign lands, we always make an effort to try the local foods. This, however, was an especially memorable experience with Bolivian cuisine.

When mentioning local foods, it is impossible to think of Cochabamba and not have popcorn come to mind. In addition to potatoes, this rich agricultural valley also raises corn, and popping corn is very popular. In fact, I have pronounced it the popcorn capital of the world.

There literally was a popcorn vendor on every street corner in and around the center of town. Needless to say, this brought on savory aromas as we strolled the streets. It was constantly being popped fresh and sold in big bags. With so much competition, the prices were very competitive and I thoroughly enjoyed the snack, particularly since I am a life-long popcorn lover. Fifteen cents bought a feast of fluffy, flavorful popped goodness.

In addition to eating, we enjoyed the sites of the Cochabamba area. A large hill adjacent to the metropolitan area was fitted with a cable car leading to the top, where there was a huge statue of Jesus Christ. Though visited by many locals on weekends, during the week, we found it to be a peaceful place to take in the vista of the city, surrounded by the magnificence of the snow-capped Andes. It was a sight to behold and I partook of this pleasure several times that week.

The military presence in the city, as well as the entire country, was a bit overwhelming. Poverty abounds throughout the nation, with the indigenous people suffering the most. However, the city of Cochabamba was a haven of relative prosperity due to its climate. Tons of fruits and vegetables are grown there. The relaxed atmosphere of the people in the streets and market of Cochabamba was very pleasant. We were able to enjoy a parade, festival, dances, music programs, and a host of locally prepared foods during our short stay of ten days.

Although our experience in Cochabamba did little to improve my expanding waistline, the potatoes and popcorn were delicious and enhanced our sojourn in this lovely city.

CHAPTER 30

The Orphanage of Trujillo

We were on a short flight from Tegucigalpa, the capital of Honduras, to La Ceiba, a small town on the northern Caribbean coast. Our initial plan had been to boat from La Ceiba to the coastal island of Utila for some snorkeling. However, while en route, we encountered many backpackers who were heading there. We have often found that backpackers can party into the night, making it difficult for us to sleep.

"I don't think we'll find peace and quiet on Utila," I commented.

Christine agreed and began reading our guidebook to look for alternative options. She found a little town on the coast called Trujillo. It sounded as if it was both quiet and quaint. The bus ride from La Ceiba to Trujillo was a dusty, bone-jarring trip. Hurricane Mitch had come inland directly over Trujillo the year before, leaving behind a path of death and destruction. Roads and bridges were washed away. We crossed through rivers instead of over them. Banana plantations were totally flattened. Unemployment was rampant as a result of the massive damage to agricultural production.

One small coastal town was completely gone, with the few remaining people moved to a new community, twelve kilometers inland. The immense amount of water left behind by the storm provided breeding grounds for mosquitoes, hence an outbreak of malaria. Christine and I were on preventive medication, but unfortunately, this was not available to many of the locals.

With all this despair, we still found the town of Trujillo to be quite nice. It is set on an amazingly beautiful bay, where we swam extensively in the during our extended twelve-day stay.

Tourists were rare in Trujillo, although we did meet a handful of North Americans who had settled there. Gringos Bar, set on the beach, was the hang out for foreigners. The restaurant and bar had an all-day feast every Sunday, which provided us the opportunity to socialize with other English-speaking people. After talking with them, we got the impression that most of the foreigners seemed to be homebodies. They usually remained in their houses in fear of being robbed. This was particularly true during the evenings. However, we moved about the town both day and night with no problem. We wondered if some of the fear was paranoia.

The most interesting group of people we met was by coincidence. They picked us up while we were walking back from Santa Fe, a small village fifteen kilometers north of Trujillo. A pickup truck, loaded with North Americans, stopped for us as we were walking back to town.

"We're from the orphanage located down the road," Joan stated.

"I didn't know there was an orphanage near here," I responded. "How many children do they have?"

"Only sixty-eight," she answered.

"We've heard of many with several hundred kids," I interjected.

"This place is kept small intentionally. We focus on trying to do a good job on the few students we have by keeping our class sizes low and providing good health care," Jane explained.

"Sounds like an interesting place."

"Would you like to visit?" Jane asked.

"Very much so!" Christine and I responded.

The next morning, we met Jane in Trujillo and she drove us to the orphanage. Upon arrival, she gave us an escorted tour of the facilities, which were most impressive. Nestled in amongst the palm trees, fifty feet from the beach, was an array of dormitories, academic and vocational classrooms, a health center with attending nurse and physician, and a soon-to-be-completed church.

The religious focus of the school was Catholic, which is the predominant religion of the area. One or two nuns taught religion while the young North American missionaries were teaching academic and vocational subjects.

The intent of the educational program was to keep the children until age sixteen, then let them out into society. The only problem was that the orphanage had not developed a transition program, which would introduce the students to the outside world. The program had been operating for twelve years, so they were about to produce their first graduates and needed assistance in getting them into the community.

Having learnt of my experience in education related to co-op programs and internships, and Christine's corporate background, we were asked to stay on for two years to help guide them through this stage of growth.

We would have been required to go through a process before being accepted to work at the institution, but it appeared that would have been a formality, as Jane handed us a multi-page pamphlet. It introduced us to the intricacies of life at the orphanage in Trujillo.

Sharing lunch with the teachers at their dormitory, we were able to explore the complexities of their two years in Honduras.

By day's end, we explained that our interest was limited, though we were quite impressed with the work they were doing with the children. This was a case where missionary zeal was truly helping people in need.

At that stage of our lives, we were not ready to settle down in one place for two years. We were too eager to see as much of the world as we could.

Our experience in Trujillo and the orphanage left an indelible impression on us. If ever we were to undertake a couple years of volunteer work, Trujillo would be foremost on our list.

CHAPTER 31

A Map for Saul

A six-hour bus ride from San Pedro Sula, the commercial center of Honduras, brought us to the lovely small town of Copan Ruinas. Arriving in the evening, we took one of the first rooms we could find.

One of the language schools in the community had been highly recommended to us by the teachers at the orphanage at Trujillo. We had inquired, as our Spanish was in dire need of improvement. We planned to spend two weeks attending classes and living with a Honduran family. A home-stay had been suggested as a highly efficient way of improving our language skills while getting to know the culture.

After breakfast, we took a short walking tour of the town and soon found ourselves at the school. Two of the owners, Hector and Patty, welcomed us. As we sat down for an extended discussion, we told them of the praises they had received from Jane and her friends in Trujillo. Over a cup of coffee, they talked about the educational center they had founded and how they could help in our pursuit of Spanish.

Encouraged by their good humor and enthusiasm, we signed up for two weeks of classes, with Hector as my instructor and Patty as Christine's. All instruction at the school was on a one-on-one basis. Our plan was to attend for four hours in the morning, leaving the afternoons free for exploring the town.

"We are also interested in a home-stay," Christine mentioned.

"We have a middle-aged couple, whose children have left. They may be interested," Patty said.

"Can we have a look before making a decision?" I asked.

"Let's meet at the school at two this afternoon. By then, I will have made arrangements with the family—for you to meet them and see the accommodations," Patty announced with a smile that seemed to say we had nothing to worry about.

We visited the home of Julia and Saul, a short walk up the hill from the school. Though Saul seemed a bit timid, Julia met us with enthusiasm and showed us what would be our room for the next two weeks. She also gave us a tour through the remainder of the house, as we would spend much time with them; our arrangement included three meals per day with the host family.

We moved in the next morning, after our first class, and thus began a very warm relationship between Julia and Christine. Although a middle-class family, with Saul owning a small coffee plantation, their kitchen remained steeped in tradition. Cooking on hot plates over an open-wood flame with passed-down recipes was the preferred method of the lady of the house. Julia was more than willing to spend hours with Christine, sharing her knowledge of cooking and Spanish. She took my wife on shopping trips to the market and introduced her to friends and relatives. It was amazing how they took to each other.

As for Saul, it was drastically different for the first few days. He remained distant, only answering specific questions and not stepping forward to volunteer information. Then on Thursday evening, after dinner, he asked, "Where are you going on Saturday?"

"We want to go to Santa Rosa and visit the cigar factory," I responded.

"How will you get there?" he questioned.

"Well, I think we'll take a bus," I hesitatingly responded, as I was not certain which bus to take or where to catch it.

He seemed to think for a bit, then responded, "It's not as easy as you think. First you have to take one bus from Copan Ruinas for about ten kilometers, then at the three-way intersection, walk to the right for a kilometer, then wait under the palapa for a second bus which will take you to Santa Rosa."

"Wait a second while I get my map," I said.

Three minutes later, I was opening a large, four-by-four-foot map of Honduras which we had purchased at the National Information Center in the capital. Laying it on the table, I pointed to Copan Ruinas and asked, "Where do we go from here?"

Saul did not immediately respond, so I took my eyes off the map and turned to him. He was transfixed on the map and had not heard my question.

My relationship with Saul changed from that moment forward. I soon came to realize that the middle-aged man had never seen a map of Honduras of this scale. Something we take for granted, a map, bewildered him. That evening, we spent a couple of hours together, discovering the route to Santa Rosa, as well as a thorough geography review of Honduras.

"It's time to go to the room," Christine said as she and Julia joined us.

"Okay," I responded while getting up from the table, not attempting to pick up the map.

Realizing what was happening, Saul began folding the map when I remarked, "It's for you to keep."

"No, no, it is yours," he said.

Upon my insistence, he kept the map and thanked me profusely. Over the next week and a half, Saul spent hours at the table, studying his map.

The minor gift elevated our relationship. He became friendlier, offering tidbits of information about his family and the coffee business.

The next afternoon, he took us to his coffee operation and to some neighboring hot springs. The following week, he took us to visit a chicken farm, vegetable farm, and to a beautiful lake at sunset, which abounded in waterfowl.

The map was the best investment I could have made for our relationship.

As my Spanish progressed under the tutelage of Hector, I was finding the four straight hours of Spanish a bit exhausting. Christine was learning at an amazing pace with the assistance of both Patty and Julia. She was clearly more into it than I was. I was impressed by the extensive conversations I overheard between my wife and Julia.

During the fifth lesson, while on a ten-minute break, I asked Hector, "Where did you get all these beautiful paintings?" pointing to a host of paintings strung about the school.

"They're all pieces of work I've done," he responded.

Jokingly, I asked, "Are you an art or a Spanish teacher?"

Seriously, he answered, "My years at university were spent studying art. I just can't make a living with my art in a small place like Copan Ruinas, so I started teaching English and now we have our own school."

His work was beautiful. He had a good command of color and technique. Having a desire to paint birds, I approached him during class for a change of syllabus. "I was wondering if you would teach me to paint birds?"

"Certainly!"

I quickly put together a plan in my mind and suggested we break up the four-hour morning session into two. "Can we do two hours of Spanish class followed by two hours of art lessons?"

"If you buy minimal supplies over the weekend, we can start on Monday," he suggested with much enthusiasm.

The next week, Hector patiently taught me the basics such as color mixing and application while painting birds. The love of a new hobby was born—one that has carried on with me. Ever since, I always have an oil brush and paint accessible. When time permits while on our travels, I partake of this very relaxing pastime.

In addition to our educational pursuits, Christine and I enjoyed taking in some of the local sites, mainly the Mayan ruins of Copan. We were thrilled to spend time at the famed archeological site, as we have both read extensively on the Mayas.

On our first visit, we limited ourselves to the Copan Museum. It provided us with an overall view of the complex as well as the underground temple. It allowed us to appreciate what cannot be fully seen on the property itself.

The second time there, we spent the day touring the ancient area. The river-front city, set in the Copan Valley, is best known for its hieroglyphic staircase on one of the main temples. Deciphering the glyphs has provided archeologists with much desired information about the Mayas and their achievements.

Our two weeks in Copan Ruinas are amongst the most memorable of our travels. While thousands of travelers go to the area for just one day to see the ruins, we were able to see the sites *and* immerse ourselves in the Honduran culture while improving our Spanish—*and* learn a new artistic hobby—*and* develop rewarding friendships.

CHAPTER 32

The Killings at Todos Santos

The Guatemalan newspapers all carried the same headlines on that Saturday morning: "Japanese Tourist and Guatemalan Guide Killed." The incident happened in Todos Santos, a remote town in the western hills of Guatemala, towards Mexico. The details were sketchy, but it seemed that an elderly Japanese man had somehow ignited a riotous frenzy among the indigenous people of the town. It resulted in the death of two people and the destruction of a tourist van.

The tragedy presented a potential problem for us, as we planned to bus from Antigua, in Central Guatemala, to Huehuetenango the following Tuesday, then onto Todos Santos on Wednesday. After a couple of days in the village, we would continue our journey north through Mexico. Our travels this particular year involved working our way north by bus from Panama to the United States over a nine-month span of time.

As a general rule, we avoid tempestuous situations, sometimes missing countries entirely when they are having major internal problems. We had read about the town in several books and had spoken to many travelers who had been there. All spoke highly of their experience and called it a true indigenous town. If we had to bypass Todos Santos, it would be a major disappointment.

The headlines in the newspapers on Sunday and Monday recapped the same story, with few additional details. Many police had been dispatched to the village and there had been no further incidents reported.

"What do you think?" I asked Christine, after she read the article.

"It's hard to say. This paper says they have closed the town to tourists. With this publicity, they may not see tourists for months. We could bus straight to Tapachula, or we could go to Huehuetenango and ask around about the situation in Todos Santos before making a final decision."

"That sounds reasonable. Huehuetenango is the closest city to Todos Santos, although it is still sixty kilometers away."

We resolved to at least give it a try and on Tuesday morning, we embarked on an eight-hour bus journey through the verdant Guatemalan highlands. The rolling hills interspersed with forest and agriculturally-developed fields were beautiful on this luxurious sunny day. Though the bus was old and on its last leg, the road was in excellent condition and we moved along without incident. By Guatemalan standards, our vehicle was considered first class compared to the chicken buses which are generally outdated school buses and crammed with people. I once counted over 120 adults jammed in an old retired bus from a U.S. school system.

The seats on our bus were rather close together, but followed the one-seat, one-person rule, which was a relief. Most buses in Guatemala do not follow such guidelines.

Checking into a hotel in late afternoon, we asked the clerk about the feasibility of going on to Todos Santos.

He thought that the town had been re-opened to foreigners but said he would check around for us. That evening, he suggested we go, as the buses were indeed taking outsiders and no further problems had been reported.

"It is an isolated incident that won't be repeated. And there are many policemen on alert in case anything erupts," he encouragingly stated.

We thanked him for his advice and went to our room.

"He hasn't totally convinced me," Christine said.

While strolling around town that evening, I suggested we give it a try. "If we sense any problem, we can get on the first bus returning to Huehuetenango."

Christine looked at me with her glorious smile and said, "Todos Santos it is."

At nine the next morning, we set off in a chicken bus for one of the most ungodly rides we have ever taken. The road was partially paved, but mostly dirt and full of potholes. Although the rains enhanced the greenery of the mountains, they also made many roads nearly unpassable. The mere fifty to sixty kilometers took about four hours. In the midst of a rain shower, we finally arrived.

The pretty town is set in a green agricultural valley, up high in the mountains. Though it did not have the standard central park of most Guatemalan villages, it did have the requisite church and market. Two things struck us as we entered the town: the very friendly people that greeted us as we got out of the vehicle, and the destitute tourist van that lay immobilized across from the market. The locals must have thrown a hundred rocks at what appeared to be a new ten-passenger vehicle. It was covered with dents and all the windows were broken.

Walking uphill, we found an inexpensive guesthouse. The owner was dressed in the colorful native garb, as were most of the townspeople. Speaking some broken English, he welcomed us to the town and assured us that all was peaceful. He introduced us to his family, suggested some hiking trails, and recommended a restaurant. He also mentioned that the market would be open in the morning and he encouraged us to have a look.

After dispatching our backpacks, we went to the restaurant and to our relief, encountered two other westerners.

"We're not alone," I observed with a smile.

"That's good. Let's have a chat with them," Christine said.

After brief introductions, I asked them if they felt safe there.

Immediately realizing our anxiety, Flora and Matt affirmed that all was well.

"We have been here since yesterday and everybody is going out of their way to be pleasant," Flora remarked.

"I think they realize that they made a serious mistake and are deeply sorry," Matt added, then went on to say, "We visited the church, market, and some shops today. Tomorrow, we plan to go hiking in the hills."

"What else is there to do?" Christine wondered aloud.

"Not a whole lot, and maybe that's the point of being here," Flora responded. "It's just a village without tourist facilities, so you just sit back and observe."

"That's why we came," Christine said, as she smiled while glancing at me.

We had a relaxed dinner and an early night. The temperatures at these higher elevations are rather chilly, and needless to say, there was no heat in our guesthouse or the other lodge in town. Fortunately, there were ample blankets and we snuggled close for a good night's sleep.

The next morning, as we walked down the main street toward the market, one of the most touching moments of our travels transpired. An elderly lady, with cane in hand and a shawl over her head, waved us to a stop. With her back severely bent over, she extended her hand up to Christine and said, "We very friendly."

Realizing the effort required for this lady to make that remark, Christine responded by giving her a big hug and thanking her profusely in Spanish. Little else had to be said and we made our way to the market.

We spent the next couple of days walking around the town and its environs. We occasionally spoke with the local people in our developing Spanish. Our observations concurred with Flora and Matt. Realizing the terrible tragedy that had occurred, the townspeople were going out of their way to be friendly.

The village had been pretty much untouched by civilization for centuries. Only over the past few years had they linked up with a modernizing Guatemala. Their mountainous location had kept them isolated and somewhat unique in the annals of our travels. We had come to see a people and village that had maintained their Mayan traditions and were fortunate to have the opportunity to experience Todos Santos.

As far as we could determine, the violence that had broken out the previous Friday was set off amongst rumors that a satanic cult of foreigners had been stealing babies in Guatemala. The elderly Japanese man went behind a mother with a baby on her back to take a photograph. This alarmed the woman and she screamed to alert her friends, igniting a riot leading to the Japanese man and tour guide being stoned to death. Evidently, the guide attempted to rescue the Japanese man, and in the process, endangered his own life. The remaining tourists ran to the bus and remained there until the police arrived. After things calmed down, the locals realized the error of their ways, albeit tragically too late.

The newspapers reported, a day after our departure, that the police had come into town at three in the morning and arrested several leaders in the attacks. Other fugitives had made their way over the hills into Mexico, according to the report.

What may have possibly further complicated the outbreak was the fact that many indigenous people believe that you are stealing their spirit when you photograph them. We always ask permission before photographing ethnic people, or for that matter anybody. The Japanese gentleman may not have asked permission to take the photo, which is unfortunate. Much of what I am reporting is based on what we were able to decipher from various conversations with locals and fellow travelers, which is hearsay and subject to question.

What is indelible in our memory is the beauty we saw in the people and village of Todos Santos during our brief sojourn.

CHAPTER 33

The Love Motel in Vera Cruz

We were heading north toward the United States, after having spent the last seven months traveling the highways and byways of Mexico with our ten-year old van. Leaving the city of Oaxaca in Southern Mexico that morning, we made it to Vera Cruz, just as the sun was setting.

Following the map in the guidebook, we drove toward the city's center. I parked the van and proceeded to find a guesthouse. After looking at several, all either dirty, without hot water, or an uncomfortable mattress, we concluded that the downtown area offered little in our price range.

"On the way into town, we passed a couple of motels that might be better," Christine optimistically mentioned.

"Okay, we'll backtrack," I hesitatingly responded. It was already dark, and we were not in the habit of driving around Mexico after dusk. On this particular occasion, we seemed to have little choice.

Within a half hour and after a few wrong turns, we found ourselves approaching the Arizona Motel. All we actually saw was a nicely lit sign. The hotel was behind a ten-foot-high cement wall.

Arriving at the office, I parked and went in to check the place out.

"Good luck," Christine remarked as I headed inside.

The front desk woman told me that she had a vacancy and would be happy to show me the room, as she led me in the direction of some twenty rooms.

Our experience in the third world had taught Christine and I to always test the mattress, ask about the hot water, and look in the bathroom for cleanliness. To this day, we stick to this policy, especially when staying in inexpensive lodging. The kindly lady showed me where I could park the van, right outside the room. She also pointed out a curtain to pull closed for privacy. I didn't pay too much attention, as I focused on the room itself. I immediately tried the mattress, which was firm, then opened the door into a spotless bathroom. Turning to the lady, I asked about hot water, to which she responded affirmatively.

Totally satisfied, I led the way back to the office and registered for the night.

Opening the van door, I told Christine, "We're all set with a firm mattress and hot water."

"That's great," my wife responded with a yawn, as she was a bit tired after the long drive.

"The room even has a king size bed and a television, although I don't know if the latter works."

"It has a king-size bed? Wow! We haven't seen one of those since we left the U.S. seven months ago," she exclaimed in amazement.

Upon entering the room and observing the quarters, she said, "It's huge! And even has a chair and desk. Not bad for ten dollars."

Lying down to retest the mattress, she looked up and laughed, "It has a mirror on the ceiling."

"It's a love motel," I exclaimed, while joining her in a fit of laughter.

Looking around the room, we found it had a rotating blind waiter for the anonymous delivery of wine. We also discovered that the television not only worked, it had an X-rated station to compliment the other offerings.

We had read in some guides that motels such as this existed on the outskirts of Mexican cities, but had never seen one or entertained staying at such a place.

My focus had been so intent on trying the mattress and looking at the cleanliness of the bathroom that I never saw the room's other facets.

I am delighted to report that the mattress was not only king size, it was also the most comfortable bed we had slept in over the past seven months. We had a great night's sleep and I was sincere when I told the attendant the next morning that we would stop in again if ever in Vera Cruz.

We still laugh when mentioning to our friends that we spent the night in a *Love Motel*.

CHAPTER 34

Driving Up the River

We had been in Mexico on several occasions and the marvelous crafts we had seen whet our appetite to see more. Cities like Oaxaca and Patzcuaro are famous for their handcrafted items, but this time around, we wanted to see what was being produced in some of the more remote villages.

We were determined that this trip would be different. For one thing, we had our own wheels in the form of a trusty old van. Additionally, we had seven months to pursue our goals. Our objective was to locate the out-of-the-way places and people we had heard about, but never had the opportunity to see firsthand.

A mattress and some kitchen essentials enabled us to sleep as campers on occasion, allowing us to spend time at some very remote beaches and villages. The van experience also helped us discover that we are not true campers, although a few years hence we did enjoy New Zealand in a full-fledged camper van with luxuries (like the ability to stand up in it) which our van did not offer. Our operation only had the basics and left much to be desired.

This was our first experiment with living the full-time life of travelers. We had set aside seven months for the trip, but never before had we been away for more than nine weeks. If it worked, we hoped to expand the experience to longer periods of time.

In addition to traveling, we were hoping to find a place where we might like to settle in the future. We were always on the lookout for apartments, occasionally renting one for a month. We frequently talked to ex-pats and retirees about the living conditions at any particular place. We stayed in Oaxaca, in Southern Mexico, for a month and also spent five weeks in Patzcuaro, which is located in central Mexico.

This particular sojourn found us taking many side trips to the various nooks and crannies of Mexico. One bright sunny day, we decided to snorkel at La Bouquilla, on the southern Pacific coast. Although highly recommended, none of our fellow travelers had been there since the advent of Hurricane Pauline.

"This dirt road is one of the best we've been on in Mexico," I mentioned while driving to the beach.

"So far…" Christine said skeptically.

Slowly, I drove downhill toward the ocean, then around a hairpin curve, when to my bewilderment, the road repairs ended and the condition of the road became a disaster.

Stopping immediately, I surveyed the situation while Christine asked if I'd be able to back out.

"It would be impossible," I said. The combination of loose gravel, a hairpin curve, and a very steep grade meant no traction. "We have to continue down to the beach and just hope for the best."

Not knowing if we would be able to get out of the mess that we had gotten ourselves into, we drove down to the beach to swim and snorkel. Trying not to think too much about the return drive, we enjoyed the activities and a delightful picnic lunch.

Finally, after several hours, I suggested that we attempt our uphill challenge.

"This road is for four-wheel-drive vehicles," my wife remarked.

"You can say that again," I responded, while slowly driving through the stream at the base of the five-kilometer hill, then gradually beginning the climb.

Having slowed for the stream, I was unable to get the head start I needed for the traction to make it up the hill.

"I have to back up, down beyond the stream, then go full-steam ahead through the brook and hope that gives me enough momentum," I frustratingly remarked as the van ground to a halt.

Having backed through the water and down to the beach, we both braced ourselves for what proved to be a roller coaster ride. Through water, dirt, and stones, we drove with all the speed we could muster. Amidst a cloud of dust, we reached the top. Though a lovely afternoon, I don't suspect we will return to La Bouquilla.

In the guide to Oaxaca State, there was a listing for an artist named Jorge Tivaca, who resided about fifty kilometers from Oaxaca City, deep in the western mountains. Oaxaca City is served with a good road linking it to Mexico City, hundreds of kilometers to the north. A paved road, in fair condition, leads to the Isthmus of Tehuantepec to the south. Going either east or west from the city is hazardous, as the mountain roads are not paved.

San Rafael, the village where Jorge Tivaca lived, was high in the hills. The dirt road began only five kilometers outside the city, which meant that we had forty-five more kilometers of dirt road ahead of us. Fortunately, it was the dry season, so the ruts were minimal and there was little mud.

"I hope this guy's artwork is worth it," I exclaimed, as we stirred up a cloud of dust, continuing our journey in the direction of San Rafael.

"According to the guide and the tourist office, he is the best painter of little figurines in the nation," Christine said. "He paints small wood carvings of Mexicans doing everyday chores."

On several occasions, we had to ask for directions, as there were no signposts. After several hours, we arrived at a small, tree-shaded village with a lady and young girl sitting on a bench beneath one of the trees. There was nobody else in sight.

We parked not knowing where to find our artist.

"Let's go ask the lady," Christine suggested.

"*Donde esta el artiste, Jorge Tivaca?*" I inquired in my best Spanish.

She consulted with the little girl, who pointed in a direction out of town.

We needed a bit more than that, so Christine went on, "*Donde?*" Where?

That was when the elderly lady surprised us with her English. "Three kilometers," she stated. "Turn left and drive up the river."

"*Muchas gracias*," Christine responded as we excitedly headed back to our van.

The old lady sitting on the bench with the young girl would have made a beautiful photograph for our album, but we had no desire to embarrass them, so we let the opportunity pass.

"I can see the photo caption," I remarked to Christine as I laughed, "The lady who told us to drive up the river."

"Let's see what the river is like," Christine said, smiling.

After a three-kilometer downhill drive, we came to the river. Since it was the dry season, there was no water flowing.

Stopping, I looked at my wife. "Shall we?" Although the river was bone-dry, the soft sand made it a questionable venture.

"Why don't we go as far as we can, then we can walk the remainder of the distance," she daringly responded.

We managed to drive a couple of kilometers on a relatively hard surface, but then the soft sand prohibited any further advancement.

"Ready to walk?" I asked, after coming to a stop.

"Not much choice," she said, as she observed that we had not seen any person or building since we left the village.

Walking approximately a thousand meters, we came to a complex of three or four houses and within minutes, we met up with Jorge Tivaca. Although his native language was Tzotzil, he spoke some Spanish and was thrilled to show us his work.

His figurines were painted in bright blues, yellows, reds, and oranges. They were very beautiful in the sunlit hut. He then directed us to his outdoor work area where we saw pieces in the making. He did both the carving, from rough-hewn logs, and the painting.

Delighted with his work, Christine selected several pieces. After brief negotiations, we made our purchases.

Turning the van around in the sandy river bottom was difficult, but once accomplished, we managed to leave the area with no difficulty.

Driving gave us the added ability to purchase items that would be nearly impossible to transport with backpacks, in addition to being able to reach places otherwise inaccessible.

We have not really had that liberty since. Traveling with a backpack limits your purchasing power significantly, which I sometimes think is not such a bad thing.

Our Jorge Tivaca figurines are an excellent representation of the fine and unique craftsmanship available in Mexico. They are beautiful keepsakes from another wonderful adventure.

CHAPTER 35

Thirty Minutes Late for a Quetzal

Several travelers had told us that Costa Rica was very expensive, while Northern Panama offered the same natural wonders for much less money and fewer tourists. Traveling from Panama City, we decided to stop in the northern city of David to have a look for ourselves. We found the place to be hot and sticky, but very convenient for making side trips.

After a short, one-hour bus ride to the cool hill town of Boquete, we found ourselves in the midst of a flower festival. Though there were occasional showers, we enjoyed the massive display of flora straddling the roaring river.

Relaxing for lunch at a local café, we met two young women travelers named Briana and Pat.

"Where else have you visited in this part of Panama?" Christine asked.

"We spent four days around the town of Guadalupe, doing a lot of hiking in the National Park," Pat responded.

"Is Guadalupe far from here?"

"Just go back to the David bus station and take a two-hour bus ride into the mountains," directed Briana. "It's the last town on the road and there is a guesthouse up there."

"Any other suggestions?" I asked.

"Not really," Pat responded. "However, we have read about a small island off the Pacific coast with a few cabins."

After our pleasant lunch and a walk around the town and its surrounding hillsides, we returned to David.

Reviewing our trusty guide that evening, we located the small island Pat had referred to earlier that day and decided to leave the next day for four days of adventure.

In effort to get to the island, we backtracked along the Panama City route for one hour, then got a ride on the back of a pickup truck to the coast. From there, a short boat ride took us to the island.

The entire island was a National Park except for the small peninsula upon which the cabins and a café were located. After dropping off luggage in our cabin, we went to the café. The German owner sat down with us over a cup of coffee, drawing a map of the island on a napkin. His crude sketch showed us where to go hiking and where to find isolated beaches.

The next morning, after a short hike through the deep green forest, we located a three-hundred-yard-long beach. The forest was to our back and the aqua blue Pacific Ocean to our front. There was no snorkeling to speak of, but the swimming was fantastic. To add to the ambiance, we were the only travelers at the beach for the entire day.

Relaxing after a picnic lunch, we both heard a loud grunting noise coming from behind us.

"What's that?" Christine asked.

"I don't know, but it sounds like wild pigs."

Throughout the next hour, the grunts intermittently occurred, progressively getting louder and closer.

Never having heard anything like it, we began a guessing game in attempt to figure out what animal was making these loud noises.

"Could it be wild cows?"

"I doubt it. I liked your pig idea better," Christine said. "Do you think it could be some sort of deer?" she asked.

"I don't know, but it's close enough to find out," I said, proceeding to get up.

Without making any noise, we made our way up the hill and through the forest, following the sound of the grunts. Within a few minutes, we heard the noise coming from overhead. Amidst the greenery of the trees, we spotted a group of large monkeys.

"Must be howler monkeys," I whispered to Christine, taking my binoculars out and listening to more grunts emanating from the trees.

"I'll get the camera," Christine exclaimed, while positioning herself under a large tree.

We devoted the next hour to photographing the slow-moving creatures.

Over the next few days, we combined hiking, bird watching, monkey observations, and beach time, for a very pleasant stay on this little island.

While returning to David, we were reading on the bus and were able to confirm that Guadalupe offers hiking and is located adjacent to a rainforest reserve. However, what really interested us was that it said the elusive quetzal could be occasionally spotted in the rainforest. The long-tailed bird is unique to Central America and is an endangered species. An opportunity to see one intrigued us both.

After a day of exploring David, we bused to Guadalupe. It was a cool village, set amongst misty mountains with a small community of vegetable farmers, a lone guesthouse, and a restaurant on the outskirts.

Checking into the guesthouse, Christine noticed on the bulletin board that cabins were available within the rainforest.

"It sounds ideal for bird watching and possibly getting a glimpse of a quetzal," I remarked.

"I'll ask at the desk," Christine said, as she headed toward the registration area. Eager to hear what was offered, I followed.

"Can we arrange for a cabin in the rainforest?" Christine asked.

"Yes. When do you want to go?" The woman questioned.

Christine quizzically looked at me, so I responded, "How about tomorrow?"

The young attendant was making notes as we provided details. I then asked, "What are our chances of seeing a quetzal while we're in the rainforest?"

"Quite good," she responded, and went on to explain, "Walk to cabin two for seven-thirty in the morning and one often feeds in the big tree immediately to the front of that lodge. There are only two cabins. You will be in number one and number two is a half mile further along the road."

"That's great! Are you sure seven-thirty is early enough to spot the quetzal?"

"Yes," she responded, smiling.

One of the most common questions among Central American travelers is: Have you seen a quetzal? The beauty, color, and grace of flight are supposedly amazing. We were looking forward to seeing our first.

At the appointed time the next morning, we met up with our four-wheel-drive jeep driver as we set out into the rainforest. Our first day was full of adventure, trekking through the jungle. What amazed us the most was the guide chopping his way along the trail with a machete, even though he had walked the path only a few days prior. Perpetual rain enables vines and greenery to inundate the trail in no time. We crossed several rapidly-flowing streams and viewed a number of waterfalls, while occasionally stopping to watch the birds. The abundance of hummingbirds, wrens, and tanagers was incredible.

Returning to our cabin, I started a fire in our wood stove while Christine prepared to cook dinner. Having been advised by the desk clerk, we brought along simple foods for hearty meals.

With a lot of dry wood at hand, we were able to heat the large cabin sufficiently to be comfortable, then retire early, by candlelight. Electricity had not yet reached the rainforest, which was nice.

"Did you set the alarm for six-thirty?" I asked Christine for the third time.

"Don't worry. We will be up in time for the quetzal," she responded.

Rainforests are known for never-ending precipitation, as our experience confirmed. It rained one hundred percent of the time we were there. The rivers roared with an abundance of water. Birds and greenery magnified the enthralling experience.

We awoke early the next morning, as planned. Within a few minutes, we had slipped on clothing and raingear, and were on our way to catch a view of the elusive bird. Upon arrival at lodge number two, we found another western couple bird watching with binoculars in hand.

"Any sign of a quetzal?" I asked.

That was when I heard the response I had not anticipated.

"Yes, you missed it by half an hour," the man said.

I looked at my watch, then at Christine. "It's only seven o'clock."

"Yes," the woman dejectedly responded. "They must have been early."

If only the desk clerk had told us six. We could have easily been there, no problem.

Spending the next few hours under cover, we enjoyed the mix of birds that visited the area, but there was no quetzal to be seen.

Returning to the guesthouse that afternoon, I remarked to the clerk that we had missed the quetzal by half an hour. She looked at me and responded with a smile, "Maybe next time."

To her, the sight of a quetzal seemed insignificant. To us, it would have been a meaningful experience that we were so looking forward to. She had no sense of our frustration as she went about her work.

We had a great time in northern Panama, with our ventures in nature, but spotting a quetzal would have been the icing on the cake. Someday we hope to have another opportunity to spot this beauty.

On a positive note, the experience did prompt a discussion and feeling of gratitude. We have been so fortunate to see and do so many magnificent and precious gifts in our travels.

CHAPTER 36

An Earthquake in Southern Mexico

At the conclusion of eight months of travel in Asia, we decided to return to southern Mexico for a month of relaxation. Logic took us back to the beaches of San Agustinillo. Having been there on several occasions, for both short and long stays, we were familiar with the area and had several friends who lived in the locale. A good rest would prepare us for work, when we returned to the United States.

The owners of the familiar *posada* greeted us with open arms, as we selected one of the rooms. It was nice to unwind in our hammocks, with the sound of the ocean in the background.

After spending several days under the shady palapa, we decided to take a day trip to Playa Ventanilla, which was only five kilometers away.

Catching a pickup truck with benches in the back, we soon found ourselves at the intersection of a dirt road that led to the beach. The driver pointed to the left of the truck and said, "*Dos* kilometers."

Walking down the road, we came across a sign, "Coconut Tortillas."

"I've never had coconut tortillas," I mentioned to Christine.

"Neither have I. Maybe we should stop and have a snack."

Under a complex housing a goat, pig, chickens, and a turkey, was an elderly woman plying her tortilla trade.

She offered us a delicious toasted sample.

Acknowledging that we would purchase a package, Christine asked the woman, in Spanish, if she would teach her the art of making toasted coconut tortillas. Without speaking a word of English, the elder took Christine by the arm and they proceeded to tamp down the mixture, forming the large, flat, pancake-like tortillas. They then placed them into the wood-fired oven for a quick turn or two. Before I knew it, I was enjoying my second coconut tortilla.

After making copious notes on how the tortillas were made, we found ourselves walking towards the beach, snacking to our heart's content.

Reaching the water's edge, we were confronted with three options: horseback riding along the beach, a canoe ride through an adjacent lagoon, or just lying on the soft white sand.

"What if we paddle the lagoon, then try the beach?" Christine suggested.

Inquiring at a hut, we found that the canoe came with a guide who presumably knew his way around the lagoon. Within minutes, he had us in the midst of crocodiles and a plethora of tropical birds. Most impressive of all were the long-tailed blue jays and the hanging nests of the Mexican oriole. An abundance of waterfowl also plied the waters.

After the two-hour canoe trip, we returned to the white sand beach for swimming, lounging, and a light picnic. I then suggested a walk along the beach, toward a rocky promontory point. Christine was agreeable and we began our stroll. We soon reached the cliffs of rock straddling the water and were forced to bring our walk to an abrupt end.

"You would need to be a mountain goat to go any further," Christine commented.

Looking up at the mass of rocks above our heads, I said, "Can you imagine what would happen if there was an earthquake right now?"

"We would be bound for another life if that ever fell on us."

By day's end, we returned to our motel in San Agustinillo. After watching another glorious sunset, we settled down for the evening, reading material in hand. Our intermittent chatting and reading were interrupted abruptly at 9:11 when the cement structure we were in began to shake. Christine and I held each other tightly until the drama ended twenty seconds later.

Looking around, we observed cracks in the wall, but the cement ceiling remained intact.

"We're lucky it didn't fall in on us," Christine commented.

"Let's get out of here in case there's an aftershock." Within seconds, we were in the parking area discussing our exploits with two other couples staying at the *posada*.

"It was over a six pointer," Rosa guessed at the intensity.

I remarked that I had been through a 5.8, which was not nearly as severe as the one we had just experienced.

Touring the rooms of the other two couples, we found our quarters had been the most severely damaged, so we moved to another room.

While eating breakfast the next morning, I suggested to Christine, "Let's go back to Playa Ventanilla and look at the status of those rocks—the ones above our heads yesterday."

"I forgot about that. I wonder if they're still there."

Walking to the street to catch a pickup truck to Playa Ventanilla, we saw Rosa. She said that she and Guillermo were heading to Pochutla and would buy a newspaper. "We want to know more about the earthquake," she stated.

"Could we have a look at the paper when you're through with it?" I asked.

"Glad to share," Rosa graciously said, while waving goodbye for now.

Reaching the rocky cliffs at Ventanilla, we found the status to be exactly as suspected. The tumultuous quake had sent the rocks tumbling into the ocean.

"Thank God the earthquake hadn't happened while we were standing under there yesterday."

Returning to the *posada* that afternoon, Guillermo hailed us over and asked that we join them for a cold beer.

Eager to fill us in on the information relating to the earthquake, Rosa stated, "It was a six point eight on the Richter scale, with an epicenter about twenty-miles off the coast."

"Any severe damage?" Christine asked.

Pochutla escaped anything serious, but Santa Maria de Huatulco was hit hard, according to the newspaper," said Guillermo.

"How much damage?"

"The church was supposedly damaged extensively and will need a lot of renovation, but there were no reported fatalities."

Years later, when visiting Rosa and Guillermo, we talked about the night of the earthquake in southern Mexico. Though not a pleasant memory, it is one we will not forget.

CHAPTER 37

The Apartment Has a Pizza Oven

We arrived in Antiqua, Guatemala, four weeks before Easter, with three objectives in mind: to take Spanish lessons, to observe the festivities of *Semana Santa* (Easter Week), and to explore the possibility of living here long term.

A day after boating and busing in from Belize, we began our quest for a Spanish school that would cater to our individual needs and assist us in finding a native family to live with.

Visiting several schools and families that first day, we felt discouraged, as the curriculum was not what we were looking for, nor had any of the families been good matches.

"Why don't I set out early in the morning to find that lady we read about—Amalia. She does private tutoring," I mentioned to Christine.

"Okay, but get back as soon as you can. I'd like to join you to look at the school on Third Avenue."

The next morning, I quietly showered as my wife rested, and by 7:30, I was on my way to Amalia's. She was reputed to be an excellent teacher who would give us individual lessons. Passing a small school on my right, while on my way to her place, I thought to myself, why not go in and see what they have to offer.

"Good morning," I greeted the middle-aged director. "My wife and I are interested in Spanish lessons."

"Let me explain to you how our system works." She then proceeded to describe the curriculum in detail.

Quickly realizing the school would not individualize the teaching for us, my eyes began to wander around the office. I noticed a small "Apartment for Rent" sign on the wall. When the time was right, I asked her about it.

"It's my father's apartment," she stated. "It's out back, behind the school."

"Could I see it?"

"Let's see if he's home," she said, while standing up and leading me out the door.

Her dad, Senor Fernando, and her mother, Anita, were in their mid-seventies. While Anita spoke no English, Fernando spoke the language fluently, articulating his words perfectly.

He told me a bit about the apartment and that it would be available the following Monday. "Can you come back at two this afternoon to view?"

"That's excellent. I'll bring my wife with me," I said, then asked, "Is it furnished?"

"Yes, and it has three rooms—a kitchen, living room, and bedroom."

Knowing how Christine likes to cook, I asked, "How well is the kitchen equipped?"

"It has everything you need—a refrigerator, stove, sink, and even a pizza oven," he answered with emphasis on the pizza oven.

"Great!" Knowing Christine made delicious pizzas, my mouth was watering at the thought.

"I'll see you this afternoon," I said, as I continued down the street for Amalia's.

As it turned out, Amalia was the perfect match for us. She would provide two-hour private lessons for each of us. Her rates were no higher than the schools we had visited and the proximity to the center of town made it very convenient.

After sharing the good news about the school with Christine, I mentioned that although Amalia did not arrange home-stays, there was an apartment nearby for rent.

"Can we see it?"

"Yes, we have an appointment at two o'clock." I went on to describe the details as I knew them. "It even has a pizza oven."

"That sounds wonderful! The market here has wonderful vegetables. We can try some new combinations. I haven't had a real oven in ages."

After a hearty lunch, we found ourselves at Fernando's house.

Upon entering the kitchen, Fernando directed our attention to the refrigerator, kitchen utensils, and countertop, which had a pair of gas burners sitting on top of it.

"Where is the pizza oven?" I asked, knowing Christine was looking forward to baking bread and making pizzas.

"It's right here," Fernando said, as he proudly pointed to a small toaster oven set behind the door.

Looking at Christine, I could see the disappointment in her eyes.

The bedroom was large and had a good, firm mattress. The living room was exceedingly small and painted black, and the television was limited to one Spanish-speaking station.

After much discussion and negotiation, we ended up taking the apartment and appreciated its prime location. During *Semana Santa*, many of the processions came by the front door.

Fernando ended up being an excellent host with even more correct information relating to Antigua and its environs than the tourist bureau. I later discovered that he had spent over twenty years employed by the tourism authority of Guatemala, which worked to our advantage and explained his intimate knowledge of the English language.

We enjoyed the world-renowned Easter festivities of Antigua immensely, with its many colorful processions, enactments of Holy Week, and beautiful *alfombras*, which are street carpets made of colored sawdust in a multitude of designs. People from all over the world came to the city for this colorful event. The city was cleaned up extensively and many homes were repainted in anticipation of the festivities. It was a memorable month and we would recommend the Easter Week activities of Antigua to any would-be traveler.

The only unfortunate incident occurred when an unsavory pickpocket made away with our credit cards, souring our experience. Upon reporting the robbery to the police, we discovered that pickpocketing occurs frequently in Guatemala. Although we loved Antigua, which is surrounded by three beautiful volcanoes and has perpetual spring-like weather, we could not visualize living in a place where we would always have to be on guard for thieves. Locals confirmed that petty crime abounds in the area. We made the decision not to remain there on a permanent basis, though we did enjoy the festivities—and the host of small pizzas from our toaster oven.

CHAPTER 38

An Airplane Ride from Merida to Oaxaca

This was one of our earlier traveling episodes, a five-week venture in Mexico. Our intent was to experiment with a travel philosophy of slower-paced, inexpensive stays, with time to experience more of the life that locals live. Arranging for our business in the United States to continue in our absence, we flew to Cancun, on the Yucatan Peninsula. We chose Cancun mainly because of the low-cost flights available from Atlanta. Merida was our city of choice, but expensive to reach by air, so after a few days on the beaches in the resort area, we bused our way inland to Merida.

After locating a clean, comfortable, twelve-dollar-per-night room, we proceeded to see the city and its environs. Buying a locally made Panama hat and hammock was a high priority and took up the better part of a day. The selection was phenomenal and the local market was engaging, as we meandered around the entire north end of the city.

Merida abounds in old churches, museums, and historic sites—which fully occupied our second and third days.

While at the bus station to head to Celestún for the day, I suggested, "We should look into buses to Oaxaca."

Although we spoke and read no Spanish at this point in time, we could comprehend enough from the marquis to understand that there was a daily bus to Oaxaca that took twenty-three hours. It left at 6:30 p.m. and cost only thirty-six dollars per person.

"The price is right, but we'll be dead upon arrival and will need a day to sleep it off," Christine said.

"Busing is fine, but we want to see Oaxaca, Puerto Escondido, Taxco, and Mexico City—all in a brief five weeks. Maybe we ought to consider flying this segment."

In later years, we have taken bus and train rides that were much longer than twenty-three hours. Though these are tiring, we get to meet interesting people and see beautiful countryside. However, at this early stage of our travels, it seemed difficult, and a mere five weeks meant we had to make the most of our time.

"Let's think it over," Christine suggested, as we boarded our bus for Celestún.

About an hour later, we found ourselves in a dream. Without another traveler in sight, we plied the waters of the Celestún lagoon in a fifteen-foot skiff, amongst a dazzling array of waterfowl. The lagoon is on the migratory route of pink flamingos, of which there were many. There were also a vast number of cormorants, egrets, herons, and pelicans. It was a photographer's dream, and our album that year shows off the amazing area.

Traversing the five kilometers to the center of town proved to be another enjoyable experience. A middle-aged Mexican, with his four children sitting in the front of his pickup truck, stopped to give us a ride. The back of the truck was loaded to the gills with coconuts.

I looked at the rear, wondering how in heaven's name we would be able to climb on board, when Christine tapped me on the shoulder, "He wants us in the front."

Crowded as we were, it was one of the most pleasant and memorable rides of my life. Staring at each other and injecting a few words here and there, though neither of us could understand, was illuminating and fun. Reaching the center of town, I broke out my wallet, but the man would have none of it. He and his children just smiled and drove off.

The coastal town was more than we could have hoped for. Looking down the dirt main road, we observed a lone man on horseback making his way through the center of town. It was a scene out of the old west. There were no vehicles in sight, though we did learn there would be an afternoon bus to Merida.

Drifting through town, we saw a large seafood restaurant facing the Gulf of Mexico. Upon entering, the owner directed us to an ocean-view table. With no other customers in the establishment, we had his complete attention.

Sitting back and relaxing to the sound of the ocean, Christine selected a seafood torta (we did not know what this was but it sounded interesting). I chose *sopa de lima*, a chicken soup prepared with special limes.

As Christine placed her order, the owner gave her a nod, saying "Number one," in his limited English. I should have guessed from his smile that she was ordering his specialty. Although my selection was adequate, her torta was an omelet and a work of culinary art. It was massive and laden with lobster tail, shrimp, and crab—incredibly tasty. To my satisfaction, there was more than my wife could eat, so I was able to indulge in the feast.

With much pride, the restaurant owner/fisherman showed us his catch from the prior evening: an array of fish and the largest lobsters we have ever seen. He was evidently pleased as we complimented him on his catch and excellent food. Who would have guessed we would have been in for such a gastronomic delight in such a tiny town?

Back in Merida, we procured tickets for a flight to Oaxaca, which was departing at eleven the next morning. The long bus ride was the determining factor in our decision to fly.

Backpack in hand, we arrived at the airport early, only to find the plane coming in from Havana was thirty minutes late.

Looking at Christine, I said, "With scheduled stops in Campeche, Villahermosa, and Tuxtla Guiterez before arriving in Oaxaca, we will probably be five hours late to our destination."

"Let's just sit and relax while we wait for the plane to arrive."

"I suppose you're right. There is nothing we can do about it anyway."

When the plane arrived thirty minutes later, it quickly taxied to our gate. Within a couple of minutes, we watched fifteen baggage-carrying passengers walk down the stairs. We immediately entered the plane and took the available seats. Without a wasted moment, the plane taxied to the runway and we were off.

At the next three stops en route to our destination, the procedure was the same—taxi to the terminal, a staircase quickly brought to the door, passengers disembark with baggage in hand, and an equal number board the plane within a few minutes.

"It's like stopping at a bus stop," I commented to Christine, as we flew off to our next stop.

"Here and gone," she remarked.

To our amazement, we arrived in Oaxaca twenty minutes ahead of schedule. I ended up eating my words. The airline was extremely prompt and efficient. It was all so simple and uncomplicated—a remarkable experience.

"Other airlines could learn from these folks," I stated, as we arrived at Oaxaca airport.

This brief holiday taught us that attempting to see such a large area in such a short amount of time can be very tiring. We were beginning to learn lessons on the art of traveling that would be of immense value when we began to travel more extensively.

CHAPTER 39

Ice Cream and Levitation

We were having lunch with James, the Canadian owner of a hotel/restaurant in Puerto Escondido, when he asked, "Have you ever been to Tepoztlán?"

"No, where is it?" I asked.

"Not far from Taxco. You should visit there while you're staying in Taxco. There's an Aztec archeological site on the high mountain adjacent to the town. It's a steep climb, but the views from the top are magnificent."

"We enjoy visiting archeological places. Is there anything special about this one?"

"It's supposedly a mystical site. People have been known to levitate while lying down and meditating."

"Levitation?"

"I know it sounds ridiculous, but I know some very sane people who claim to have levitated on that mountain," James said. "Another good reason to visit Tepoztlán is the ice cream."

"Ice cream? Is it safe to eat?" I asked.

We hesitate to eat ice cream in third-world countries because freezing, unlike boiling, does not kill the bacteria that causes dysentery. A fellow traveler had become severely ill after eating ice cream in Delhi, which made us all the more cautious.

James continued, "It's very safe and the ice cream parlor is right on the main street, so you can't miss it."

"Ice cream and levitation it will be," exclaimed Christine, as we bid farewell to James.

While relaxing at the beach the next day, Christine searched through our Mexican guide for information on Tepoztlán. Although ice cream was not mentioned, the adjacent mountain and archeological site were recommended.

"Looks like there are a couple of inexpensive guesthouses," Christine said. "Maybe we could stay the night and get an early start to climb the mountain in the morning. It's listed as a very steep climb so we better wear our climbing shoes." This was a joke as we each travel with just one pair of multi-purpose shoes and shower shoes.

After leaving the beach, we traveled to Taxco to view the festivities of *Semana Santa*. The Silver City, as it is often called, is known for both its silver mining history and the religious processions preceding Easter. As we anticipated, the city was jammed with people from Mexico as well as foreign tourists. The hotels and restaurants were filled to capacity. It was one of the few times in our travels that we made hotel reservations in advance, and we were glad we did. The two-week stay gave us ample time to get a good flavor for the celebrations, along with the opportunity to shop for gifts of silver. The city must have hundreds of jewelry stores plus loads of local craft merchants setting up shop on the streets during the religious festivities.

On one auspicious morning, we awoke to the yelling of "*Agua, agua,*" coming from the street below.

We opened the balcony door and found open trucks packed with youngsters. They were all looking up, "*Agua, agua.*"

We figured that they were coming in from surrounding villages, literally by the truckload, to participate in the festivities.

"I think they want us to throw water on them," Christine remarked.

"You're right. Let's oblige."

From our second story balcony, we proceeded to throw water at the young merry makers.

When glasses full of water did not placate them, we began filling the wastepaper basket.

With traffic moving at a snail's pace, we were able to give many of them a soaking. Residents and hotel workers from across the road had joined in on the fun and we all had a marvelous time.

The processions were much more somber than our experience with the young folks. Long lines of penitents, dragging chains and carrying racks of thorn-ridden reeds on their back, mark many of the parades. There was also a fair amount of self-whipping, with people drawing blood as a result of the self-infliction.

Scenes from two thousand years ago were recreated as part of the activities, all of which added to our memories and photo album. *Semana Santa* in Taxco was an interesting time for us and I would recommend it to any traveler.

When the festivities subsided, we proceeded to Tepoztlán. We spent the night at a two-room guesthouse located in the center of town, so we could get an early start for our mountain climbing venture. Simple directions from the hotel owner had us at the base of the mountain within a few minutes.

Christine and I are not hikers, so what might take athletic types an hour, took us several hours. We were amazed to find locals who actually climb the mountain several times in one day for the exercise. Slowing our ascent was our penchant for marveling at the scenery above and below. In some areas, the climb was steeper than we had anticipated and we found ourselves climbing up ladders.

The view from the top was striking, as it overlooked the valley below with the pretty town in its midst.

The archeological site was well preserved, though we questioned why it had been located at the top of such a high mountain.

"Maybe levitation had something to do with it," I suggested, as we maneuvered our way to the temple.

We reached an area where several foreigners were attempting to levitate while lying in a meditative mode. Respecting the others, we quietly agreed to give levitating a try.

"Who knows? Maybe it will work."

For all our efforts and those of our fellow travelers, we did not, nor did anybody else on the mountain, levitate that particular day.

The descent was actually more difficult than the climb, although less tiring. We had to be careful not to slip on a rock or twist an ankle while stepping down.

We were glad we got the early start because by mid-afternoon, there were many people climbing the mountain. We practically had the mountain to ourselves, except for the half dozen people on the summit.

Reaching the town center, we immediately headed for the ice cream parlor and indulged in a well-deserved treat. They offered a multitude of flavors in an array of colors. We relaxed with our choices, under the shade of a canopy. The strawberry flavor was delicious. Christine's flavor, called "kiss of an angel" lived up to its name.

It was a pleasant way to conclude this travel episode. Although we did not manage to levitate, the scenery from the mountain had been magnificent and the ice cream was the cherry on top.

CHAPTER 40

Teaching Koreans in Guatemala

After much deliberation, we decided to return to Antigua, Guatemala and give ourselves a second chance there. It was possible that the pickpocket had jaded our view of the beautiful city during our earlier visit, so we decided to try again.

Once we found an adequate apartment, we hoped to further explore Central and South America. It was now January and we wanted to settle by April. We would take a furnished apartment as soon as we arrived in the city and then search for something that would be appropriate for the longer run. We thought we might remain for a few years, using it as a base for travel.

Upon arrival, we took a room in a small hotel and spent the first few days checking bulletin boards, newspapers, and asking around in search of an apartment. Initially, our efforts were in vain. Then one morning, as I happened by the bulletin board at a grocery store, I noticed an ad for a furnished three-room apartment in the market area. I began writing down the details when I noticed, out of the corner of my eye, a second ad for a school in search of an English-as-a-second-language teacher. Thinking it over, I decided to make note of the information regarding the job opportunity. I had spent four years, while in my twenties, as a teacher and had enjoyed the profession very much. I wondered if it might be a good idea to return to the classroom.

Joining up with Christine later that morning, we searched for the posted apartment, and although not quite to our satisfaction, we decided to rent it out on a monthly basis. The flat had its own foibles. For one thing, the rooms were set out in the same procession as railroad cars—you entered the living room, then had to go through the bedroom to get to the kitchen. Additionally, the shower only put out cold water, and there were so few windows that we had to have the lights on even on a bright sunny day. On the plus side, the kitchen was relatively well-appointed by Guatemalan standards, and most important of all, there was a four-burner stove with a full-size oven. The miniature pizza oven we had on our previous stay in the city was nothing compared to this.

Within a day's time, we had unpacked our luggage and stocked up on our basic food necessities.

"I might like to follow up on that teaching job I read about the other day," I mentioned to Christine.

"Sounds good. You may very well enjoy teaching again."

"It will give me something to do while we search for a more permanent place and while you take your meditation course," I added.

Christine was planning to participate in a full-immersion, month-long yoga and meditation program at Lake Atitlan. She would live at the meditation center for that entire period of time with no return trips to the city.

Antigua is small for a city, so I had no difficulty walking across town the next morning, in search of the English school. After an interview with the director and then the owner, I accepted a position teaching five hours per day, beginning the following Monday.

"How old are the students?" I asked Teresa, the director of the school.

"Most of your students will be in their early twenties."

"How many students per class?"

"You'll have two classes with five students each. The remainder of your time will be teaching one-on-one to Korean students," she explained.

"Korean students?"

She must have sensed my surprise. Before I could inquire further, she continued, "Yes, many of our students are from Korea. There are about sixteen thousand Koreans who live in Guatemala. Most of them reside in Guatemala City and the parents send their grown children here to learn English."

"That's interesting. What are they doing in this country?"

"The parents are owners or managers of factories involved in the garment industry."

"Why do they only begin to learn English when they are twenty years old?"

"The students remain in Korea while the parents live here. After they graduate from a Korean university, they move to Guatemala."

"Why do they study English and not Spanish?" I further questioned, as my curiosity was beginning to pique.

"Some also study Spanish, but most prefer English because it is considered the international business language," she explained.

"They must be motivated students."

"Yes, they are very motivated. You'll find it a pleasure teaching them," she concluded, as a bell rang announcing the end of classes.

With books in hand, I bid farewell to Teresa.

Upon returning to the apartment, I proudly announced to Christine, "On Monday, I begin my new job teaching English to Korean students."

"Korean students?" She was surprised, just as I had been.

"Yes," I responded with an explanation of the circumstances.

The next couple of months went by quickly.

Christine enjoyed her meditation program, although I missed her dearly. We haven't spent much time away from each other since our marriage, never mind an entire month.

I kept myself occupied with oil painting and teaching English.

The Korean students were indeed motivated young adults, preparing to embark on careers. Teaching one-on-one, I got to know the few students very well. In addition to our educational association, they introduced Christine and I to Korean cuisine and I even did some hiking with several of them. Our friendship became long-term, and in a subsequent year, we were able to spend time with them while visiting South Korea.

My small classes of Guatemalan students were also very rewarding. All were young adults, preparing for careers requiring English as a second language.

We spent three months in Antigua that year. We were able to find a nicer short-term apartment with grand views of the surrounding volcanoes, but decided it was time to embark on our travels to South America.

CHAPTER 41

A River Runs Through Our Kitchen

Over our years of travel, Christine and I have had a number of furnished apartments for brief periods of time. They provided us the opportunity to get to know the communities better, catch up on daily routines, and enjoy local markets. However, taking apartments in the third-world can have its ups and downs.

Noise is often a factor that we've had to adjust to. The first morning at any apartment is always interesting simply to see what will serve as our alarm clock. The most notable wake-up call was at a second-story apartment we stayed at in Mexico—where a church, only three hundred yards away, rang its bells at six o'clock each morning. Much to our dismay, we have learned that roosters actually begin to crow before dawn; in fact, it is usually around 3 a.m. Dogs can and do enter into fits of howling at any hour of the night. Our current apartment, north of Bangkok, has a lovely river view, but the sound of riverboats is always present during the early morning hours. With all of these potential sleep disturbances, we have gotten in the habit of using earplugs. Although not foolproof, they ameliorate the situation.

Several of our apartments have been large rooms that are subdivided by the furniture. The kitchen is where the stove, sink, and refrigerator are situated, while the location of the bed determines the bedroom. We have adapted to this rather well as long as the room is large enough to accommodate our needs.

Location is always important to us, as we enjoy having a view. On several occasions, we found ourselves with magnificent panoramas. One of the most striking views was of the three volcanoes from our balcony in Guatemala. The slow-moving red glow of lava flowing from one of the active volcanoes was simply stunning on clear evenings. On the other hand, we once had an apartment with no windows, which felt very enclosing. Our view over Lake Patzcuaro was great, though we suffered from haze on many days.

Electricity, which we often take for granted in the west, is not always as consistent in other parts of the world. One apartment had us losing electricity every evening between seven and eight, while thunderstorms often brought disruptions in Guatemala.

The number of electrical outlets can also present a problem, as there are almost always too few. Often, we have had to buy extension cords with multiple outlets to alleviate the problem. In fact, Christine has become very adept at flicking the switch of our multi-plug adapters with her toes, as they usually have to be placed on the floor due to insufficient counter space. What can be frustrating is that these same outlets frequently burn out. Using more than one appliance at any one time can become problematic, as it overloads the system. One time, we caused the outlet to melt simply by leaving a small cooler plugged in for thirty days. We felt bad for the landlord, but we certainly didn't anticipate that usage for a month would be hazardous.

Living with little or no counter space or kitchen cabinets has also become standard fare. Kitchens in Thailand usually come totally unequipped, if there is a kitchen at all. Thais eat out regularly since street food is so inexpensive. A refrigerator and hot plate are the most that they might offer, just to accommodate snacks and breakfast.

We also had to scale down our expectations regarding the size of refrigerators in furnished apartments. They nearly always come with a unit about half the size of those in western homes, with the freezer space being extremely limited. Back in the United States, we had a double door refrigerator as well as an additional freezer in the garage. Fortunately, most of our apartments have been in close proximity to a market, which enabled us to shop frequently. The abundance of fresh fruits and vegetables helps to make up for the lack of refrigerator space.

Shopping can be both a challenge and delight. Markets offer unusual fruit and vegetables. We have tasted and enjoyed mangosteen, an Asian fruit which Queen Victoria longed for so much that she offered a reward for anyone who could deliver a fresh one to her. The reward was never given since England was too far away in those pre-flight days. We don't consider ourselves picky eaters, but durians are a fruit we strongly dislike. They're also called stink-fruit—a name they live up to.

Some things which are luxuries in North America are plentiful and cheap in other parts of the world. In Thailand, we can buy crab, shrimp, red snapper, and asparagus for a fraction of the price elsewhere.

Finding the right ingredients can be challenging. Buying flour and yeast for homemade pizza can sometimes require locating a restaurant-supply store, as Central Americans and Asians do not routinely bake bread. Some toppings can be easy to find and very inexpensive; but others, like real parmesan, blue or goat cheese, sun-dried tomatoes, or oregano—end up costing a premium. Another hard-to-find treat is my favorite apple—a good, crisp granny smith; that has been a holy grail search in most Central and South American countries. Although, in Thailand, I have found excellent ones—thanks to imports from Australia. I also miss drinking lactose-free milk. I love milk, but my body does not. The solution in the United States is Lactaid. I search for it wherever we stay more than a day. So far, I have only found it in Singapore, where I made up for lost time by drinking a liter a day for the week we were in that city-state.

One summer, we rented an apartment in Oaxaca, Mexico. It was very well furnished, and with a unique kitchen, in that it was outdoors. An overhanging cover offered protection from sun and rain. We actually found it quite nice. Fortunately, this apartment complex was not inundated with mosquitoes or flies.

The only problem with the open-air kitchen was that we were there during the rainy season. The showers often came in the early evening, when Christine was preparing dinner. The overhang kept her dry from the rain, but the water run-off followed its natural downward trajectory—through the center of the kitchen.

I was listening to the pitter-patter of a heavy rainfall one evening, when Christine dashed into the living room exclaiming, "There's a river running through the kitchen!"

"What do you mean?

"Come and see," she responded.

Sure enough, there was a three-foot-wide stream of water going right through her work area.

After informing our landlord about the problem, he installed a downspout to direct the water away, while I created a small dam with bricks to redirect the remaining water. However, both of our efforts proved to be in vain during heavy showers.

We learned to live with it and now laugh about the river running through the kitchen.

That same apartment was very quiet, as the owner did not permit dogs or roosters in the complex and the nearest church was quite a distance away. The only exception was the night that Vincente Fox had won the election as Mexico's new president. The roar, fireworks, and band music were so great that every corner of the city reverberated with excitement. It was a thunderous occasion for a people desirous of change.

On our travels, we have marveled at the excellent food that can be produced with little to no equipment. We have eaten well in Mexican restaurants equipped with only two gas burners, or a charcoal fire, topped with clay plate. We have seen plastic buckets used as mixing bowls or to wash the dishes. In Indonesia, a small brazier can cook the food while a clay pot and wood pestle are used to mix the vegetables and sauce for the famous *gado-gado* (salad with peanut sauce). Having to work with what is available, we have used a pint-sized electric kettle to cook meals like shrimp and vegetables.

Sometimes, it is the simplest things, like preparing a meal, that can lead to the most interesting experiences. The many kitchens we've lived in have given us numerous challenges, but also many happy memories—while we hoped to not get electrocuted or nuke the wiring.

CHAPTER 42

One Hundred Ten Countries After Sixty-Two

During our years of travel, we have had the pleasure of meeting many interesting people. There were two couples we dined with at a small restaurant in Northern Bali, who rank as some of the most captivating. We had seen the elderly couple, Edna and Mike, several times around the village, but never had the opportunity to speak at length. Recognizing us as we entered the restaurant, they invited us to join them.

"Where are you two travelers from?" asked Mike.

Christine explained that she was originally from England and that I was from the United States. She added that we had been in Thailand, Malaysia, Singapore, and Indonesia over the past four months.

"Where to next?" Edna inquired.

"A month in Australia, a month in New Zealand, followed by Fiji, then a couple months in Mexico," I said.

This was our second year of travel and for a couple in our fifties, Christine and I were both proud of our exploits.

"How about you folks? Where are you traveling to?"

"Now that we're in our eighties, we don't travel nearly as much as we once did. We're spending two months in Indonesia and then returning home to Australia," said Mike.

"It sounds like you traveled extensively in the past."

"Actually," Mike stated, "I have been to one hundred ten countries since I retired at age sixty-two."

The statement got our attention, for the elderly couple were alert and could be a wealth of information for want-to-be travelers like us.

I was curious to see how well his memory served him. "Have you ever been to the States?" I asked

"Yes, I spent two years traveling there in '83 and '84," he responded.

"I'm originally from the Boston area," I said. "Did you go to that city?"

"Yes," he said, "I was there for a couple weeks one summer and really enjoyed it. I stayed at the Bradford Hotel, just south of the Boston Common. It was rather reasonably-priced."

Christine and I looked at each other in astonishment as he recalled his travels in such detail.

Christine asked, "Do you mind if I take out a pencil and paper to take a few notes?"

"No, go right ahead," Edna chipped in.

In the course of the evening, we bombarded him with questions. We were planning a trip from Panama to Mexico for the upcoming year and he had made the same trip fifteen years ago, so we had many questions. Where did they snorkel in Belize? How was the food? Are there inexpensive places to stay in Panama City? Was Costa Rica as expensive as they say? What hotel did they stay at in San Jose?

His memory was excellent and his answers precise. Never before had we encountered any traveler as informative as this gentleman.

As it happened, he and Edna had always wanted to travel, but were limited on time because of their professions. Once retired, they embarked on a series of low-budget trips. As the years wore on, Edna sometimes remained behind, but Mike continued his globetrotting.

One extensive voyage took him from Helsinki to Moscow and then on the Trans-Siberian railway to Beijing. From there, he headed west to Tibet, then down to Katmandu—all in the course of a year. Neither of us had ever been to either Russia or China, so our ears were open to everything he said.

An hour must have passed. Just as we were about to order, a third western couple entered the restaurant.

Never one to shun company, Mike asked them to join us. After a slight delay, we all ordered at once.

They introduced themselves as Allison and Hans, from Germany.

Christine asked them what they were doing in Bali.

"We've come to this area of Bali for two months, each of the last eight years," Allison responded.

"Why do you always come to this town?" I asked.

"I'm an anthropologist doing fieldwork in an indigenous village up in the mountains. We stay here while I do my research," Allison responded.

"How about you, Hans?"

"I'm just along for the ride."

As the next two hours proceeded, we amassed an amazing amount of information. Allison had much information to impart about Indonesian culture, and in particular, details regarding an isolated hill tribe beyond the scope of travelers.

With reservations, she told us how to find the village. She suggested we visit—as long as we follow her restrictive guidelines.

Several days later, we rented a jeep and were able to make the trip. We were amazed that such an isolated group of people could still reside on an island as densely inhabited as Bali.

Allison had warned us that as a result of centuries of inbreeding, we would see both physical and intellectual defects. She had also suggested that we look at the faces of the young and old, to notice the differences made by a more nutritious diet. Indeed, human disabilities were visible and seemed to be present in abundance. The elderly had pinched, narrow features while the younger people had fuller faces. Being in the mountains, this isolated group had little access to protein until the late twentieth century.

Near the end of the evening, we agreed to meet Edna and Mike at a later date. They seemed to enjoy talking of their travels and we were happy to continue collecting data for our future travels. Allison and Hans were returning to Germany the next day, so it was the first and last time we were to meet with them.

I expect the food was probably good that evening, although I have no recollection of what we ate. It was the company we shared that will be forever cherished. It felt incredible to intermingle with the two inspiring, informative, and genuinely nice couples.

Mike became our traveling role model. We have never set a goal for the number of countries that we would like to visit, but one hundred ten sounds like a good figure. We would love to be as energetic and enthused about life as Mike when we are his age.

CHAPTER 43

Emu Oil

Having arrived in Alice Springs, Australia, after a twenty-six-hour bus ride from Townsville, we rested in a comfortable room above a local pub. Early the next morning, we boarded a tour bus, which would be our mode of transportation to visit the big Red Center of this large nation.

Once on the coach, we were greeted with ten friendly people emanating from all corners of the globe. The first leg of our journey took four hours and brought us to the massive rock outcroppings called the Olgas. At one point, the bus driver announced, "We're about to do something significant." Now with everybody's attention, he went on to say, "We're taking a right turn." This part of Australia is arid and barren. The roads are straight for hundreds of kilometers with nothing to see but desert.

With many hours on the bus, we began talking with Sandra and Ed, a very likable Australian couple in their mid-sixties. Over the years, they had visited many places in the world but hadn't seen much of their homeland. Presently in retirement, they were making up for lost time, seeing Australia. Over the next several days, we became good friends with these lovely people.

Christine and I seldom join tour groups. Usually, guided travel expeditions move at a quicker pace than what we like.

They are also typically more expensive. However, the Red Center was different than most places, in that it would have been difficult to do on our own, and likely, less cost-efficient.

This tour would provide us with the opportunity to see Ayers Rock (a lifetime goal of Christine's), the Olgas, and the chance to hike the circumference of Kings Canyon. The latter being the filming site of *Priscilla Queen of the Desert*—a movie with cinematography we both admired.

Later that afternoon, as we were hiking in the vicinity of the Olgas, Sandra mentioned that Ed had open-heart surgery the previous year, so they would have to fall back.

"We should slow down too. My arthritis is acting up," I remarked.

"If you get stiff, let me know," Ed said, "I have a bottle of emu oil."

"What does emu oil do for arthritis?" I wondered aloud.

Over the last ten years, I had done a lot of reading about arthritis, but had never heard of emu oil as a remedy. On the other hand, I am not one to discount natural remedies.

"It's good for muscle stiffness, but it helps arthritis too."

"If it gets worse, I'll try it," I acknowledged with thanks.

After watching the sun set over Ayers Rock, we enjoyed a pleasant dinner with Sandra and Ed. The resort restaurant allowed us to grill emu, crocodile, and kangaroo steaks over an open fire. The meat was complemented by salad and vegetables. Eating our feast outdoors under the amazing star-filled sky made for a most enjoyable evening.

Our new friends offered a host of suggestions for Southern Australia, in particular, the Melbourne vicinity. South Australia was our next stop, so their advice was welcomed.

"Be certain to rent a car and drive the Great Ocean Road," Sandra recommended.

"How long will it take to drive?"

"One day's driving from Melbourne will take you to the most picturesque portion of it," Ed stated.

This particular suggestion was most welcome, as we later discovered the southern coastal road has some truly magnificent scenery. It is one of the most beautiful drives we have ever taken.

Up at five the next morning, we were soon on board the bus headed for Ayers Rock.

"Are you going to climb the Rock?" Sandra asked.

"Yes, I want to see the sunrise from the top," I responded.

"It's too much for us. We're going to stay with the bus as it circumnavigates the Rock," Ed proclaimed.

Christine looked to Ed and said, "I'm with you."

By 6:15, we were at the base of the rock. I departed the trio and began to ascend the monolith. Fortunately, there were chains straddling the steeper portions of the trail—a godsent to help me pull myself up. Tired and well worn, I reached the top by sunrise and was able to watch the bright red globe come up over the desert. It was a work of art, as it reflected off the distant Olgas—a sight I shall never forget.

The descent down the massive outcrop was worse on my muscles and ankles than the climb had been. I was very stiff when I rejoined Christine, Sandra, and Ed, two hours later at the bus.

Immediately recognizing my problem, Sandra asked, "How about rubbing in some emu oil after that climb?"

Why not? I thought to myself. It can't hurt. "I'm game." I raised my trouser legs and took off my shirt.

Ed had evidently anticipated my need and had the bottle ready.

Christine did the honors, covering my arms, back, shoulders, and legs with the oil. She rubbed it in well but hastily, as we were about to embark on our bus journey to Kings Canyon.

"Thank you very much," I said to Sandra and Ed, appreciating any assistance my body could get under these circumstances.

"Delighted to help," Sandra responded, then added, "Did I mention that emu oil sometimes has a mild aroma that begins to develop after you've had it on for about an hour?"

Not smelling anything at that moment, I remarked, "Thanks for the warning."

An hour later, as we were busing toward the canyon, I began to smell the not-so-mild odor.

Quietly, I leaned toward Christine and asked, "Do you smell the oil?"

"How could I not?" she responded. "It's very, very strong."

To say that emu oil has an objectionable odor is putting it mildly. I could sense that the smell had enveloped the entire bus.

"That emu oil does have a slight smell to it," Sandra interjected from the adjacent seat.

"I hope you feel better, Richard," Ed chipped in. "It's worth it if it helps."

Christine and I responded with smiles, trying to mask our discontent.

By the time we arrived at Kings Canyon, we were relieved to hear our first stop was at the resort. I quietly leaned toward Christine and said, "I'll take a quick shower as soon as we get to the room."

"Good idea!"

By now, I was certain the entire group was eager to see me leave the bus and get to a shower. The smell had become oppressive.

Unfortunately, it took several showers before the odor was completely gone.

Sandra and Ed had been sincere in trying to help and were delightful traveling companions, but this was one time I could have done without the natural remedy. Whatever benefit I derived from the emu oil was overridden by the horrible smell.

The next morning, we hiked around the outer perimeter of Kings Canyon. Though the walk was done under the duress of muscle and arthritis pain, I never asked Ed to open the bottle of emu oil.

Kings Canyon was as beautiful as the depictions in the movie, and we were happy to have seen the Red Center of Australia. It was unquestionably worth the time and distance to see the center of this marvelous nation. The natural beauty of the area was breathtaking.

CHAPTER 44

The Brown Rice of Lombok

Some thirty kilometers east of Bali, Indonesia, is the beautiful island of Lombok. Though only four hours away by slow ferry, the island is dramatically different from Bali in both flora and people. Dominated by the large volcano, Gunung Rinjani, the climate is generally much drier. While the inhabitants of Bali have a culture with their own version of the Hindu religion, Lombok has a Muslim based culture, as does most of Indonesia. The economy of Bali is mainly fueled by the tourism industry, with some agriculture, while that of Lombok is an agrarian society.

We planned to stay at a bungalow in the resort area of Senggigi, using that as a base from which to see the island. After two days of relaxation on the beach, we treated ourselves to an outstanding three-dollar massage by a wizened elderly man with magic hands. Muscles now relaxed, we rented a jeep and set out to tour the outer perimeter of the island. Stopping at some of the small villages, we were able to see and buy some of the local handcrafted pottery for which Lombok is noted. Christine was particularly interested in the home-spun brown pottery. The indigenous weaving was beautiful and we thoroughly enjoyed watching the weavers work their looms.

Most travelers go to Lombok to climb the volcano and take in the magnificent views in the early morning, but my arthritis put restrictions on such a venture. The snorkeling around some of Lombok's outer rim islands was superb, and we were more than satisfied to partake in that activity. Sadly, much of the coral has been destroyed, though the fish were brilliant.

While relaxing by the waterfront one afternoon, a German couple suggested we eat at a nearby restaurant, where travelers congregate at seven each evening.

"You have to sign up in advance, in order to have dinner with the group," Elga informed us.

"Is it family-style?" Christine asked.

"Yes, and you usually meet interesting people from all around the world," Tim added with his heavy accent.

Looking at my watch, I asked, "Is it too late to sign up for tonight? It's three o'clock."

"No, but you better hurry."

Without hesitation, Christine and I were off to make our reservation.

The set menu was a mix of Western and Indonesian foods. That evening, the chicken satay would be enhanced with the famous Indonesian peanut sauce and accompanied by local spinach and brown rice.

As we registered for the meal, the receptionist noted that this was the only restaurant on the island that served brown rice. She added that it was one of the specialties of the house and travelers seemed to really like it. We had not had brown rice since leaving the United States months ago and were looking forward to it. Indonesian restaurants serve different varieties of rice, though most are white. Although the restaurant was a bit expensive for our budget, at almost two dollars each, we were happy to sign up for the meal.

That evening, we had a fine time chatting with two French people who had recently been snorkeling at the Togian Islands, around northern Sulawesi. Another woman, Jane, was on the trip of a lifetime. This was her first time in the third-world and the next day, she would be departing to do volunteer work at an orphanage inland. Her plan was to spend a month working with the needy. She was probably in her mid-forties, and had spent several years saving for this altruistic venture.

She stated, "I've dreamt of this most of my life and I'm really looking forward to meeting all the children."

It was clear that anxiety had built up in her, as she was very nervous about the entire episode. Never having left England before, Indonesia was very strange to her, never mind an orphanage out in the wilderness.

All of the guests could sense her worries and tried to calm her with much optimism.

Many Dutch travelers visit Indonesia, and we were happy to mingle with a young couple from Holland. They had just biked the island of Flores. It was a place we hoped to travel at some point, so this was a good time to explore the idea.

"Did you climb Keli Mutu Volcano and see the colored lakes?" I asked.

"Yes, they're beautiful, but be sure to get up there early for a better chance of clear weather," they both admonished.

"What else did you enjoy about Flores?" Christine asked.

"Don't miss the Komodo dragons on Rinca Island."

"I thought they were on Komodo Island?"

"They are, but Rinca is a better place to see them. We saw eleven of them, while other travelers we met had only seen two on Komodo Island," he stated emphatically.

"Is the snorkeling any good around Flores?"

"The best snorkeling is off the north west coast."

Our questions went on and by the time the evening was over, we had pages of notes which ended up being extremely helpful several years later.

The food had been good, enhanced with great conversations, and the brown rice had been excellent, just as the receptionist had promised.

Two evenings later, we returned for a second meal, to find that Jane had already returned from the orphanage. In tears, she described the pesty mosquitoes, the chickens and pigs running around loose, and the straw mat that functioned as a bed. The combination of howling dogs and crowing roosters had kept her up all night, further amplifying the situation.

We all empathized with her and did our best to provide a shoulder to cry on. It had been a very traumatic experience for her. Jane had left England ill-prepared for the third-world, much less an isolated orphanage with hundreds of children in the hinter lands of Lombok.

We all agreed with her plan to return to England on the next available flight. A young British traveler agreed to accompany her to a travel agency the next morning—to assist in arranging alternative flight arrangements.

The next day, we were relaxing at the beach in our hammocks, when Christine said, "Listen to this…"

"What is it?"

"Let me quote you from the book I'm reading about Lombok Island: 'You will find brown rice raised throughout the island for animal consumption. It can be purchased inexpensively in twenty-kilo bags. White rice is raised and sold for human consumption throughout the island and costs much more.'"

"At least it was good," I responded, in the midst of an uproar of laughter. "Have we been taken or what?"

"Maybe, maybe not. It's a matter of perspective. We paid for a meal that included brown rice and good company—and that's exactly what we got."

Returning to Bali, we mused at our travels on Lombok, which included good snorkeling, meeting great people, buying beautiful handcrafts, and eating the favorite food of the local animals.

CHAPTER 45

The Hole in the Road

The Island of Flores was foremost on our minds as we visited Indonesia for the third time. Nearly all the travelers we met who had been there stated that it was the most beautiful island in the archipelago.

After spending a brief time in Bali, we caught a short flight to the town of Ende, in the center of the elongated island of Flores. After landing, we walked out of the small airport and located a truck heading east. The two-hour journey through the green mountains took us to the small town of Moni. The winding mountainous road was very scenic and beautiful, as we had heard. Arriving at sunset, we quickly set about finding lodging for the evening.

The town is little more than a one-kilometer street with a series of guesthouses and restaurants which accommodate mainly hikers and mountain climbers.

We immediately confirmed with the matron of our guesthouse that a truck would be driving up Keli Mutu Volcano at four in the morning. Although many backpackers hang around Moni for several days, our intent was to stay the night, view the volcano and its colored lakes at daybreak, then head west to see other parts of the island.

Early the next morning, Christine and I found ourselves on a bench in the rear of a truck. We snuggled together in effort to counter the cold mountain air. The damp chill of the early morning and the switchback road made for a rather unpleasant ride. We arrived near the summit within half an hour in the mist of dense clouds—which restricted visibility to ten feet at most. The sixteen hundred meters of elevation had us in a difficult predicament. Fortunately, Christine had thought to bring a flashlight, which helped us scale the last kilometer in darkness.

Sitting on stones waiting for the sun to rise, we heard voices approaching from a distance. To our surprise, two other couples were coming up the trail. Chatting with the four people, we discovered they had rented a jeep for the ascent and then planned to drive back down the mountain. We planned to descend on foot, to further enjoy the scenic countryside.

"Is there a trail leading to Moni?" one of them asked.

"Yes," I responded, recalling what I had read in a guidebook.

"How long of a walk is it?"

"Only about seven kilometers. It shouldn't take more than a couple hours."

"Sounds like fun. Too bad we have a vehicle."

As daybreak approached, we found our way to one of the colored crater lakes. It was evident by now that there would not be a scenic sunrise on this particular morning. We were still in the density of clouds. Through the mist though, we did manage to see the green, blue, and black lakes in the midst of a rugged moonscape setting. Though cold, we enjoyed the magnificence of the natural geographic phenomena.

By 7:30, Christine and I energetically set off to find our way down the mountain on foot. We followed the path to the road, then proceeded for approximately two kilometers. We then saw a hand-made "Moni" sign and an arrow directing us to a path on the right.

"I guess that's the way," I stated.

"Looks like it, but that's a meager excuse for a sign."

We agreed to give it a try. If the path ended up being a disaster, we could simply return to this point and walk down the road. According to what we had read, the path was shorter and much more scenic.

Soon we were below the clouds and passed several locals working their patches of garden.

"Moni?" I asked for confirmation, and they pointed down the trail.

An hour later, we found ourselves in a small, mountain village. Locating an inhabitant, I again asked, "Moni?" He too pointed toward the path leading down and around the mountain.

Three hours later, we were going through fields and villages, with the locals continually confirming our direction. Although we were enjoying the scenic beauty of our trek, my arthritis was beginning to seriously hamper my ability to walk. Five hours and about twenty kilometers later, we finally arrived in Moni. Walking down the mountain had raised havoc with my legs. We had made a mistake that would make it difficult for me to walk over the next few days.

Both agreeing that I would be better off at a lower and warmer climate, we picked up our pack at the guesthouse and boarded a bus heading west toward Bajawa. The eight-hour trip over mountains and coastal road provided great scenery through the winding terrain. Realizing my difficulty in walking, the bus driver kindly dropped us off at the door of our desired guesthouse in Bajawa. Christine quickly made arrangements for our stay of several days, which would hopefully provide ample time to recover.

Late the next morning, Christine said, "I think I'll take a walk around town and try to find the local market."

"I wish I could join you. Maybe I'll sit in the shade in front of the hotel and read."

After breakfast, Christine headed off, as I sat to take in a good book.

Several hours later, Christine had not returned. I thought to myself that she must have found the market interesting. She enjoyed shopping in local markets, so I thought nothing of her being gone such a long time. It was very much like her to become engaged in the energy of a bazaar and lose track of time.

Much later, and much to my surprise, a local dropped her off in front of our lodging. She slowly limped toward me. Seeing the bottom of her leg wrapped in gauze, I asked, "What happened?"

"I was walking down the street, looking at some of the adjacent stores, when I fell into a four-foot-deep sewer hole," she responded with a smile on her face.

"Really? How bad is it?" I asked, as we hugged.

"The gash went down to the bone and I needed twelve stitches. A local man saw my plight in the hole and helped me out and drove me to the hospital."

"How was the care?"

"It was very good. They cleaned it out well, stitched the wound, and I am now on antibiotics. The only thing I didn't like was the line-up of huge crickets sitting on top of the screens in the hospital room—they must have been five inches long. Anyway, then they found me a motorbike taxi to bring me here."

"Hopefully the antibiotics will take care of any infection," I optimistically stated.

Within a couple of hours, the smile came off of Christine's face, as the injection wore off and she found herself in great pain.

Both of us sat around Bajawa for the next few days, giving our bodies a chance to recover.

At one point, Christine remarked, "Do you remember the lady in Oaxaca?"

"What lady?"

"On our first trip to Mexico, you asked an elderly North American woman for her advice on living in Oaxaca."

"Yes, I remember. She told me the most important thing about living in Mexico is to always look down at the sidewalk because there could be a hole in it."

We both laughed, remembering the old woman's suggestion. Christine added, "I should have followed her advice."

"Yes, it definitely applies in Indonesia too." I reminded Christine of friends of ours who returned from the Dominican Republic. They were disgusted and swore never to return due to the potholes in the sidewalk. With that school of thought, there would be very few places to satisfy.

We remained in Bajawa for four days and then took a six-hour bus journey to the coastal town of Labuan Bajo.

After several days in this beautiful harbor village, Christine went to the local hospital and had her stitches removed. Albeit, we both had doubts about the cleanliness of the local medical facilities, Christine healed remarkably well and with little infection. We had heard that wounds take longer to heal in the tropics, with an enhanced chance of infection, so we were satisfied with her progress. Christine also helped the cause by taking very good care of the wound with the help of good old-fashioned iodine.

With the removal of the stitches, we employed a boat to take us to a remote island, two hours north of town.

Renting a hut for five days, Christine rested in a hammock under the shade of a tree, while I did a lot of snorkeling. The doctor had advised against going in the water for the next two weeks, so she was not able to join me in my underwater exploits.

Despite our mishaps, we enjoyed Flores very much, and felt it lived up to its reputation as the most beautiful island on the Indonesian archipelago. Next time, we just need to look out for huge holes in the road.

CHAPTER 46

Two Paintings for a Lipstick

Who are the nicest people you have encountered in your travels? It's a question we've been asked many times and we always consider the citizens of Myanmar (formerly Burma) a close second to those of Bali.

Mandalay, a city in Myanmar, inhabits half a million of the most pleasant people you could ever hope to meet. We even considered a six-month stay, and might have done so, if it were not for the complexities of obtaining a long-term visa.

Having taken in many of the city's restaurants, temples, and cultural programs, we decided to explore some of the outlying villages. We had read about a series of ornate temples about fifteen kilometers south of the city, so one early morning, we caught a bus heading in that direction.

We must have unknowingly miscommunicated our destination to the driver, because we were dropped off at the wrong place. We could not speak the local language and the driver could not speak English.

Without another bus, truck, or automobile in sight, we began walking in a southerly direction toward where we thought was our destination. We enjoyed our walk in the country, admiring the rice paddies running parallel to the Irrawaddy River. With April temperatures in the nineties and only an occasional motorbike passing, we were fortunate to spot a picnic table beneath a large banyan tree. Without hesitation, we decided to take a break.

A smiling woman greeted us and understood our sign language, which indicated our desire for a cold drink. By the time the drinks arrived, we were in the company of the woman's husband and their six children. Five minutes later, the grandmother arrived. Despite the fact that we spoke only a few Burmese words and they only knew one or two English phrases, we managed a one-hour conversation. Sign language, pointing, and gesturing enabled us to develop a brief friendship. After several photographs, they provided us with an address, requesting us to mail the photos once they were developed.

Utilizing sign language, they managed to inform us that the temples we wanted to see were only a few kilometers down the road. Bidding our new acquaintances farewell, we began to walk along, only to find a man working on his rowboat beside the river.

"How would you like to take a boat ride on the Irrawaddy?" I asked Christine.

"Why not?" And we turned to head toward the fellow and his boat.

After a few minutes of gesturing and negotiations, the man gave us a tour of the area in his man-powered boat. We ended up giving him more money than he had requested. The downstream portion of our sojourn was a breeze, but it took a substantial effort to get us back upstream.

After visiting the temples, which were small in stature when compared to those we had seen in Rangoon and Mandalay, we continued our trek down the road. Walking in parallel with the river, we eventually came to a park overlooking the water. Places like this may be crowded on a

Sunday, but on this weekday, we practically had it to ourselves. The place was delightful, with monkeys and birds in abundance on the riverfront setting.

Seeing a kilometer-long footbridge crossing the lagoon, Christine suggested we walk across while looking out for photographic opportunities.

At a small shaded overlook in the center of the bridge, we encountered a middle-aged woman painter. Using a combination of ink and watercolors, she was creating a lovely landscape painting. She asked if we had any interest in buying a piece of her work, to which we responded, "No, thank you."

A short while later, Christine mentioned that she quite liked the artist's work and may in fact like to purchase a painting.

"I wonder how much she will charge for her art." Christine said.

"I don't know, but without any prospective customers in sight, she might be reasonable. We can stop by on our way back."

On our return, the lady asked once again if we wanted to buy a piece of her work.

This time, we stopped and spent about fifteen minutes looking at her paintings. We really liked two of her pieces and selecting the preferred of the two was difficult.

Determined to solve our problem, she handed us the two, suggesting we buy them both.

Deciding on our first choice, Christine pointed to it and asked, "How much?"

The price was higher than we had anticipated and five minutes of negotiating left us miles apart.

Finally, the woman asked, "Have a lipstick?"

Christine caught on immediately and within a few seconds, I realized what was happening. She wanted to trade a lipstick for a painting.

We had read that when traveling in Myanmar, one could effectively use lipsticks as bargaining tools when negotiating in a market. Even to this day, when walking through markets in third-world countries, Christine carries a spare lipstick. Costume jewelry also works well on occasion.

In Myanmar, good lipsticks are not generally available and are highly prized by indigenous ladies.

Always prepared, Christine took out an unused lipstick from her handbag, indicating she was ready to talk business. Examining the item carefully, the lady looked up at us with a broad smile.

Without further ado, the lady placed the lipstick in her pocket, and to our surprise, began to package the two paintings.

Looking at Christine, I said, "Two for one?"

"Who is complaining?"

Shaking hands, we thanked the lady profusely and she did the same in return. Presumably she was delighted with the trade, and needless to say, we were certainly pleased.

Our journey to this area had involved a lot of walking, which we wanted to avoid on our return trip to Mandalay. Beginning our departure from the park on foot, we saw a young man with a horse and buggy, off in the distance. As we approached, we realized he was running a taxi service. Knowing what we wanted, he offered to drive us to a village, for what we considered to be a high price. We were more than willing to pay though, considering the heat of the day.

"A lipstick will not work with this fellow." I smiled at Christine.

To which she laughed and agreed.

After a two-kilometer buggy ride, we transferred to a truck which was transporting people to Mandalay.

Some days are unexpectedly perfect, and this was one of those days. A short excursion to see a few temples ended up being a series of wonderful experiences with some lovely people. It was far beyond anything we had anticipated.

CHAPTER 47

A Day on the Irrawaddy

Limited to a twenty-eight-day visa to see a country like Myanmar, we had to move along at a quicker pace than what we typically like. We would have enjoyed remaining in Mandalay for more than a week, but we still had Bagan, the massive archeological site, and the Inle Lake area to visit before returning to Rangoon.

We did consider ourselves fortunate to have four-week visas. Only a couple of years prior, travelers had been limited to fourteen-day visas, which was scarcely enough time to see Rangoon and Bagan.

How to get from Mandalay to Bagan was the question at hand. We could fly, but that would be too costly. As for the buses, we found there was an all-day, second-class bus making the journey, but that was not ideal either.

"The couple on the train mentioned a boat that plies the waters between Mandalay and Bagan," Christine mentioned.

"Let's ask at the hotel. A boat sounds better than an old broken-down bus."

The hotel desk clerk told us where to inquire at the river harbor. He further suggested we pursue it immediately, as there were only two boats per week that made the voyage.

Walking among some twenty to thirty-foot cargo boats, we came to a large three-deck boat that looked like it had been around since the 1920s. In fact, it had probably been built by the British during the colonial era. Although aged around the edges, it seemed sturdy enough to make the trip on the quiet river.

"If we do take this boat, I'd like to get here early so we can get a spot on the upper deck. The views will be great from up there," I stated.

Christine pointed to a little shack near the dock. "Let's get some information."

"Hello, do you speak English?" I asked upon approaching the booth.

The man responded by pointing to an old sign painted in English.

"Looks like Tuesdays and Thursdays at six-thirty in the morning."

"Tuesday is tomorrow. I see why the hotel attendant wanted us to get here right away," Christine said. "Let's ask if we can get advance tickets."

I asked the attendant about buying a ticket now, while pulling money out of my wallet.

"No, no, no," the man responded as he pointed toward the 6:30 sign.

"Okay, early it will be—if we want to beat the other travelers to the top deck."

We left our hotel at 5:30 the next morning and took a bike rickshaw to the waterfront. We used the same driver that had been transporting us around town all week. He was reliable and more than willing to get up for this early departure. In fact, he always seemed to be there when we needed him. One evening, he waited for two hours while we attended a puppet show. Like most bicycle rickshaw drivers, he was lean and muscular, due to his profession. But the best part about him was the warmth he extended to us. He had us at the docks in no time flat and we rewarded him handsomely for his devoted service.

The ticket booth was open and there was a little activity around the boat, which we took as a good sign. Greeting us with a handshake, the same ticket salesman sold us our passage and directed us to the vessel.

"We're the first ones on board," I mentioned to Christine, as we balanced along an eight-inch plank onto the boat.

"Great! We can get a good seat."

Making our way to the upper deck, we found that it was just that—a deck only. There were no chairs or benches in the vicinity.

While putting down our packs, I said, "I saw a couple of chairs on the second level as we were coming up the stairs. Give me a moment and I'll see if I can scrounge something up."

Within a few minutes, we were seated on white plastic chairs, awaiting departure amongst increased activity below.

The upper level was quite small, with only enough room for a dozen or so chairs, if there had been that many on board. Fortunately for us, at the center of this deck was the control room, which provided shade as the day wore on. We simply moved our chairs around in effort to stay in the shade.

At precisely 6:30, the vessel departed. As we were leaving, a French-speaking couple from Paris walked up to our upper level. Utilizing our infrequently used French, we invited them to join us for the day. They gladly accepted our invitation and I indicated where they might locate chairs.

Although our French has its limitations, and Francois and Irene spoke no English at all, we ended up having some very pleasant conversations as the day progressed.

They were in Myanmar for the extent of a twenty-eight-day visa, but had been in the nation longer than us and offered suggestions for our sojourn to Inle Lake.

Although the boat did not provide any facilities, except for a basic restroom, we had a wonderful day. The Irrawaddy River is the mother river of Myanmar. It begins in the northern mountains and meanders south through the center of the country. By and large, it was one kilometer wide for most of our twelve-hour journey.

After leaving Mandalay, we only came across five or six small villages over the several-hundred-kilometer trip. We made four stops that day, with no stop lasting more than ten minutes.

During that brief period of time, a plank was thrust from shore to ship, a handful of locals got off or on, and cargo was unloaded or taken on. The cargo consisted of basic items like coconuts, bags of rice, and vegetables. The entire village seemed to be at the pier for the boat's brief stop; much of the town's commerce was conducted during those few moments. The items being loaded or off-loaded, were handled by a human chain. Bags of rice were handed from one person to the next until the task was accomplished. Meanwhile, a host of vendors were selling items such as steamed corn and rice cakes to the few passengers on board. The entire commotion was a ready-made scene for a turn-of-the-century movie feature.

The land itself was parched, as this was the hot, dry season. April is the hottest month in Southeast Asia, although the breeze over the water made it bearable. As we looked over this vast land, it was clear that many of the fields were unused and becoming overgrown in what had once been the rice basket of Southeast Asia.

The entire day's journey was truly a trip out of the past. It was like stepping back many decades. The rolling hills, meandering river, and smiling indigenous people brought us back to an era gone by for much of the world. Christine and I considered it a privilege to have experienced a day on the Irrawaddy.

CHAPTER 48

A Tibetan Monk in Southern India

Christine had read about the Sera-Je Tibetan community in southern India and thought it would be worth visiting while we were in the country. It was one of the refugee camps that had been established when the Tibetans were run out of their homeland by the Chinese.

"It's about fifty miles west of Mysore," Christine stated, as we were being jousted about on a bus going from Mangalore to Mysore. The sub-par road made the trip rather uncomfortable as we went from the south coast to the south-central city. Trains had been the most comfortable means of transportation in India, but the Mangalore to Mysore track had never been completed. Although the ride was difficult, the scenery was beautiful as we passed through the southern mountains.

"Maybe we can take a day trip from Mysore to visit the Tibetans," I suggested.

"That sounds like a good idea, but I think we should spend a night in order to get a real feel for the place," she added.

"Do they have sleeping facilities?"

"I think so."

Six hours into our "five-hour trip" with still another hour to get to Mysore, the bus slowed down as we pulled into a small city. Seeing a sign over a bank, I blurted out, "This is it!"

"This is what?" asked Christine.

"It's the place where Sera-Je is located. Let's get off here. It'll save us from having to backtrack from Mysore."

I must admit that in addition to wanting to see the Tibetan settlement, I was more than happy to be done with the bus.

Quickly gathering our things, we stepped off the bus, not having any idea what to do next.

"Why don't you sit and enjoy a cup of coffee in the bus station, while I scout out the town and see if I can figure out how to get to the monastery," I suggested.

"Sounds great," Christine said, as we made our way to the restaurant.

Once she settled in, I headed out, not knowing how long I would be gone or what to expect. Rounding the corner, out the front door of the bus station, I came face to face with a Buddhist monk. He was dressed in the typical burnt-orange robe and had a shaved head. Without hesitation, I stopped him and requested assistance.

Speaking excellent English, he responded, "Yes, I can help you get to Sera-Je. Are you alone?"

"No, my wife is in the restaurant with our luggage.

In the rush of obtaining information, I had forgotten to introduce myself. "I am Richard," I stated, while extending my hand.

"I am Gywye," he said with a smile.

Christine was astounded to see me return so quickly. She was even more surprised to see me accompanied by a Tibetan monk.

As we joined her for a cup of coffee, Gywye explained that he would get us a taxi and give the driver specific instructions to get to the Sera-Je guesthouse. He informed us that we would be able to eat at the lodge and then identified sites we might be interested in visiting within the Tibetan village.

"That is great! Thank you so much," I said in appreciation.

"Tomorrow morning, I will meet you at nine o'clock and give you a tour of the entire camp, if you would like," he offered.

We hesitated to respond, not wanting to take advantage of his generous hospitality. However, with a bit of coaxing, we agreed to meet as scheduled.

Gywye got us off on the ten-kilometer ride to the guesthouse. Arriving at the entrance to the village, we were astonished at the change of environment the moment we entered the Tibetan enclave.

The cleanliness and hospitality were truly amazing. Having become accustomed to India's persistent touts and beggars, we enjoyed the feeling of peace and relaxation that permeated this complex. The contentment was absorbing and made a permanent mark on us.

We soon settled into the living quarters, then ate a good meal. For the remainder of the evening, we strolled around the Tibetan town, relishing the tranquility.

After a good night's sleep, we were excited to meet Gywye at the appointed time. For the next two days, we thoroughly enjoyed his company and hospitality.

Over several thousand acres, the Tibetans had established a semi-autonomous community over the past four decades. Massive temples had been built to accommodate the religious needs of the ardent followers of the Dalai Lama, while agricultural development enabled them to meet their nutritional needs. In addition, there were hospitals, stores, markets, schools, retirement centers, and everything else necessary to sustain the thousands of refugees.

In spite of all these efforts, it was clear that they had a strong desire to return to their homeland. Centuries of living at cool, high altitudes with lower oxygen made it difficult for them to adjust to the heat and lower altitudes of southern India. Nevertheless, they had made the best of what India had provided, by developing these refugee camps into wholesome living areas.

Gywye brought us to his home and introduced us to his friends and his parents. He had made the arduous journey across the mountains with his uncle five years earlier when he was fourteen years old. His parents had left Tibet two years later, when they knew he was safe. His father was a bright-eyed man with a marvelous smile. Gywye also introduced us to his fellow monks at the monastery. The rigors of years of meditation and study were described to us as we listened to the chants.

On the second day of our escorted tour, we rented a taxi to view the outlying facilities, which included agricultural stations and several small Tibetan villages.

Our two days at the camp were most memorable for the peace and quiet these people were able to establish in the midst of a hectic and chaotic world. Gywye had introduced us to a different culture with its own way of living and we were grateful to have met him.

One of our goals, which we hope to accomplish later this year, is to visit Tibet and its people. We are interested in seeing first-hand, the land that brought forth this peace-loving society.

We kept in touch with Gywye for several years after our visit. In his last email, he told us that he would be returning to his homeland. Unfortunately, that meant that we would no longer be able to communicate with him via the internet. Someday, we hope to receive another email from Gywye, the Tibetan monk from southern India, and rekindle our friendship.

CHAPTER 49

A Protein Feast for Ten Dollars

Our friends from Oaxaca, Mexico, Ed and Nora, sat down and gave us detailed notes on travel in India. They had lived in Goa for three years and traveled extensively in South Asia while Ed was employed in that part of the world. We talked for hours with them, taking in every bit of information they had to offer.

"What about eating and health?" Christine asked. We had heard of many travelers becoming severely ill while traveling in India, and had met one lady who had been hospitalized with a severe stomach ailment.

"We would advise avoiding meat, anytime or anyplace, and you should be okay," Nora suggested.

"You mean become vegetarian?"

"Yes, they handle meat differently than we do in the west, so it's better to stay clear of it. They have excellent vegetarian food and it's safe to eat," Ed added.

"Should we stay clear of ice cream?" I inquired.

"Yes," he responded without hesitation.

Although my wife and I are not big meat eaters, we do enjoy chicken, fish, seafood, lamb, and the occasional turkey dinner. We were used to having protein in our diet, so going vegetarian would require some sacrifice. As for vegetables, we both love them and consume more than our share—and the idea of adding lentils for protein was not detrimental to our appetite.

During our trip to India, we had followed Nora and Ed's advice. We had not eaten meat since our departure from England, which included nine weeks in India, one month in Nepal, and four weeks in Myanmar. The dietary program worked so well that we stuck with it during our travels through Nepal and Myanmar. Neither of us suffered from any stomach ailments during that period of travel and we became accustomed to the non-meat regimen as time went on.

Now we were in familiar Thailand, and although we continued on the vegetarian diet, we had no reservations about eating meat in that nation.

"Take a look at this ad," Christine exclaimed, while reading the Bangkok Post. "A restaurant at the Dusit Thani Hotel is offering an all-you-can-eat buffet lunch for ten U.S. dollars—and that's for two people."

"I wonder what it includes." Not having indulged in a western all-you-can-eat meal for a long time, my interest was considerable, especially since the Dusit Thani is a four or five-star hotel that augured well for its restaurant. It was an elegant place that exuded quality.

"According to this ad, it includes lobster, several styles of shrimp, smoked salmon, crab, and grilled fish."

"We'll have to give it a try," I said. "I'm ready for some heavy-protein eating."

Christine agreed and further suggested that we go on Tuesday, since it would likely be less busy.

The lunch special was from 11 a.m. to 3:30 p.m., so we decided to arrive at approximately noon to enjoy a slow, deliberate meal that would extend over several hours.

Upon arrival at the restaurant, we were seated and offered an invitation to look over the buffet.

"Let's check it out before we commit," I suggested to Christine.

I should explain that in our travels, we very seldom spend five dollars each for a meal, and considered this to be a splurge. We knew that it would be a bargain by U.S. standards, but we were in Thailand and five dollars is a fair amount of money in that country.

Our brief stroll by the food layout had our mouths watering. A buffet of equal offering at a first-class hotel in the States would have set us back thirty to fifty dollars per person.

The ad in the Bangkok Post had not mentioned the rack of lamb, roast beef, grilled chicken breast, a multitude of salads, vegetables, potatoes, and cheeses. All of these items were in addition to those listed in the newspaper—but did not increase the price.

Sitting back down, we discussed strategy while sipping a cold drink.

"No bread or potatoes for me," I said.

"You're right," Christine elaborated. "Let's save space for the protein."

"I will have some vegetables, though."

"Did you see the desserts?" Christine asked.

"No, but I'll pass on those too."

"Not me," she said. "I'm going to save some room for that chocolate mousse."

With no further encouragement, we began to engage in our fantasy meal. Lobster tail, shrimp, and lamb were my favorites, while Christine enjoyed all of those and encouraged me to try the smoked salmon. Her advice was welcomed and I indulged with a touch of dill.

Needless to say, the next three hours enabled us to make up for any protein deficiencies we may have suffered over the past several months. We left at three o'clock, stuffed to the gills—and I even tried the chocolate mousse.

The Dusit Thani lived up to its reputation of a superb hotel with a great restaurant. As for Christine and I, we did not eat again until evening—the following day.

CHAPTER 50

Tri Binh One

This story goes back to my days in the Marine Corps and the Vietnam War. I spent much of 1965 and early 1966 on a series of operations and patrols in the vicinity of Chu Lai, Quảng Ngãi Province in the northern portion of South Vietnam. A number of the patrols were in the environs of a village called Tri Binh One. The small hamlet of several hundred inhabitants had an agricultural orientation with a special focus on raising sugar cane and rice with the addition of some animals—chickens, hogs, and the occasional water buffalo. Interspersed amongst the thatch huts were small vegetable gardens with sweet potatoes and squash.

This small settlement was about ten kilometers north of Quảng Ngãi City, the provincial capital, as well as a refugee center during the early stages of the war.

Fast forward to the summer of 2001. Christine and I are traveling through Vietnam from south to north, on a thirty-day visa, which meant we had to move along in effort to meet our traveling goals. Thirty days is not nearly enough for a nation of this size. Our trip from Ho Chi Minh City (also known as Saigon) to Hue, in the center of the country, was via minivans and buses. From Hue to Hanoi, we traveled by train.

As part of this trip, I wanted to stop by Tri Binh One, and locate the area of the Command Post from which we had operated.

Our bus was traveling from Nha Trang to Hoi An. On this particular July day, we got off when the vehicle was driving through Quảng Ngãi, during the late afternoon. Although a fairly large provincial capital, we located only two possibilities for lodging in this very non-touristy city. At the northern end of town, there was a nice but rather expensive hotel, and in the center of the city was a run-down trade union hotel. Operating on limited funds, we decided to stay at the trade union facility. We were only able to locate one restaurant that was open in this city of fifty thousand people, but the food—spring rolls, fish, and rice—was delicious.

Early the next morning, we set out to find personalized transportation to help us locate and visit our desired destinations, then drive us an additional fifty kilometers north to Hoi An. Motorbikes and drivers were readily available and inexpensive. However, we questioned the dependability and safety of the particular cycles we examined.

"Let's try the big hotel," Christine suggested. "They should offer something reliable, though it may be expensive."

The receptionist, who spoke limited English, confirmed that the hotel would rent out a jeep and driver for our one-day trip. It would take us to Hoi An and stop wherever we would like along the way. The fee of thirty-five U.S. dollars was very high for Vietnam.

"Maybe we should get a bus to Hoi An, and forget my personal ambitions," I suggested.

"No, this is a once-in-a-lifetime opportunity and I think we should take it." She was insistent.

I agreed, and within thirty minutes, we were on our way.

The driver, who spoke minimal English, did not relate to our request to find Tri Binh One. It occurred to me that the local names for villages could be different from those on the topographical maps utilized forty years ago. Refusing to give up, after our efforts to get this far, I decided to rely on my own geographical instincts. I had the driver turn off Highway 1 when I thought we were in the approximate vicinity of Tri Binh One. We traveled on this dirt road for several kilometers until the road narrowed to a mere path.

"This is the area. Let's get out and walk," I excitedly suggested to Christine.

In very little time, we reached the hamlet of Tri Binh One. Much was the same as it had been. We observed Vietnamese ladies sifting rice along the pathway, using hand machinery and wearing what we used to call black pajamas, paired with the traditional conical straw hat. Showing them the camera, they agreed to photographs, so Christine clicked away as I observed and joined in with them.

Departing this scene and going further into the village, we encountered a young Vietnamese man who spoke some English. Explaining that we were just visiting the hamlet, he kindly invited us to his family home.

Using him as an interpreter, we spent the next hour chatting with him and his family, while enjoying a glass of their homemade rice wine. Once again, we took a series of photographs to commemorate the occasion, which we later mailed to the young man.

The biggest changes that had occurred over forty years were the presence of electricity and the large sugar cane processing plant. Other than that, the place was pretty much the same, though much more peaceful.

As for the people, we found them to be remarkably friendly, considering the circumstances of my first encounter in the 1960s. With all being apparently forgiven, we had a very pleasant time with them.

We traveled further north in search of the command post area. Although only several hundred yards off the main road, it was difficult to find because the area had changed substantially. Back in the '60s, there was not a building in sight of the compound, and now, the road was lined with homes and businesses. Identifying what I thought was the approximate area, I asked the driver to pull over. Christine and I then embarked on our explorations. After some walking and shuffling about, I was able to recognize a pond which we marines had dug out to get water for showering. I was surprised to find that alongside what had been our compound, was now a sand and gravel operation. Another change was that the massive field area that had served as a landing zone for helicopters, was now overgrown with trees making the site all the more difficult to find.

With no people in sight, I proceeded to locate the vestiges of my former headquarters. Christine was amazed at my ability to locate the exact locations of the various components of our battalion.

On our onward voyage to Hoi An, I reflected with Christine about my various experiences in the area. What probably struck me the most was the beauty of this entire coastline. I had seen it years earlier, but never appreciated it. I had been so occupied with the efforts of war that I failed to see what was immediately before my eyes. I was also impressed with the degree to which these enterprising people had developed their nation in such a short span of time. In just over thirty years, they had gone from a war-torn divided nation, to a united progressive country.

Our visit to central Vietnam and Tri Binh One was a very rewarding experience, while bringing back memories of the past. At the conclusion of the day, I was glad that Christine had encouraged me to pursue my goal of revisiting the two vestiges of my past.

CHAPTER 51

Spotting Rhinos in Nepal

Nepal is noted for the Himalayas, in particular Mount Everest. Many visitors to the kingdom partake in trekking as a means of immersing themselves in the country's beauty.

What many people do not realize, is that although the country is known for a host of peaks that exceed twenty thousand feet, the southern portion of the nation that borders India is a mere three thousand feet in elevation. Proceeding north from the Indian border, the elevation rises dramatically.

In the grasslands of southern Nepal lies Chitwan National Park, with an array of wild animals that most people tend to associate with southern India or Africa. Our friends Nora and Ed, as well as several other travelers, had suggested we stop for a break at the park after leaving India. There are a number of small guesthouses in the town adjacent to the park and it would be a relaxing interlude in the midst of a heavy travel schedule. After nine hectic weeks in India, Christine and I were both for it.

We arrived in the village in the darkness of early evening. The lack of streetlights made it difficult to find a guesthouse. Once we succeeded, we approached the owner, who asked us where we had come from.

"We've spent the last couple of months in India," I answered.

"How long do you have in Nepal?"

"About a month," Christine responded. "Why?"

"I know everybody wants to go on a safari in Chitwan, but I would suggest you hold off for a couple days. You both look very tired and may want to relax a bit," he said.

"We are. Maybe we'll take your advice. We just need some time to think about it."

Rising as late as ten o'clock the next day, any lengthy activities were out of the question. We decided to see the town and ask about elephant rides and jeep safaris into the park.

Stopping at several agencies that offered elephant rides, we discovered that the cost of such an escapade was the equivalent of twenty U.S. dollars per person.

"That's a crazy price," I said. "They want to get rich overnight." The value of money is very different so this rate seemed very high for this part of the world.

"Let's forget about the elephants and concentrate on a jeep safari," Christine suggested.

"Ed told us jeeps were the best way to spot wild animals because of the massive distances involved. They cover a lot more area in a shorter period of time," I explained.

"I wonder what it costs for an all-day jeep safari," Christine said, while noticing an agency up ahead.

Once again, the best price we could muster was twenty dollars per person, but we seemed to be getting more value for our money in an all-day safari, versus a two-hour elephant ride.

We signed up for a safari for the day after next, and planned to spend an additional day lazing around.

As Christine napped the following afternoon, I went on a short hike into the park. With it being the dry season, I was able to cross the adjoining river on foot. After crossing, I walked parallel to the river for several kilometers, following pathways within the eight-foot-high grass, then turned inland for another kilometer or so. I spotted no wildlife except for a myriad of birds, but did encounter several herds of water buffalo with their attendees. Without exception, all three herdsmen waved for me to return to the village. They were very insistent, though they spoke not a word of English. Being ever curious, I did not heed their advice and proceeded further into the park.

Returning to the lodge later that afternoon, I found a note from Christine. It stated that she was wandering around town. A bit tired myself, I decided to relax on the veranda. Half an hour later, she strolled up, beaming.

"You'll never guess what happened …while walking down the street, I encountered a man riding on top of an elephant, so I stopped him and asked if he would take us for a ride, and guess what…"

"He said yes?"

"Yes, and for one dollar!" she added.

"When do we go?" I asked, suddenly interested.

"Later this afternoon. It will be a sunset ride. We'll meet him at the very place I met him on the street."

I should explain that it was not out of the ordinary to run across an elephant on the street in this little town. There were probably as many elephants as dogs. What *was* surprising was the agreed upon price of one dollar. We concluded that the driver was making money on the side while the owner of the elephant had no knowledge of the escapade.

The elephant driver met us as agreed and took us for a very pleasant ride through the village, across the river, and into the grasslands for an exquisite sunset ride. We did not see any wild animals but we were enthralled with the excursion.

Returning to the guesthouse after dinner, we relaxed while reading the local newspaper. To our amazement, we discovered that a local buffalo herder had been attacked and killed by a tiger the previous day. Now I knew why the herders were anxious for me to leave the park while on my lone trek that afternoon. Needless to say, that was the last time I explored Chitwan without a guide.

Our jeep driver picked us up at six the next morning for our safari. Early morning was supposedly the best time for spotting wildlife. The jeep was an open-air, six-seat vehicle, with a driver and professional spotter in the front. We were in the middle seats with another western couple in the rear.

Tigers were rarely seen on these excursions, although an occasional rhino could be located, as well as an abundance of deer and some crocodiles.

With binoculars and camera at the ready, we set off for our adventure. During the first ten kilometers, we spotted numerous deer but no rhinos. Not wanting to be disappointed, I decided to stand myself, to see what I could spot.

Within five minutes, I quietly exclaimed, "There's one," while pointing to a rhino on my right. It stood about fifty meters away in the tall grass. This ended up being our first of seven rhinos we saw that day. Unfortunately for the spotter, he had managed to locate only one of the seven, while I had first sight of the remainder. Christine and the other couple encouraged him all day, so as not to embarrass him, while I kept my eyes peeled for the elusive animals. We also saw crocodiles, monkeys, and lots of bird life that day while traveling fifty kilometers through grassland, dense forest, and jungles. We had never seen rhinos in the wild and were elated with the opportunity.

Though the guide did very little spotting, he did dispense a wealth of information about the animals and plant life, making our day at Chitwan National Park another engaging and enjoyable day.

CHAPTER 52

Mount Everest for Christmas

Not only do relatives have difficulty buying Christmas gifts for perpetual travelers, we also have problems buying gifts for each other. Several years back, we decided to gift each other special travel related adventures, that we otherwise would not undertake. We had read and heard about ninety-dollar flights over Mount Everest and we both had a keen interest in seeing the mountain from that vantage point. The problem was budgetary restraint, which was psychologically overcome when we decided to give each other the flights for Christmas. The trip to Nepal was already on the agenda because of its proximity to India. The bonus would be Mount Everest.

With every country we visit, one of our objectives is to get off the tourist track at least once, in an attempt to see how people live without the insulation of tourism. Gorkha was our choice for Nepal. It sounded interesting, though we had not met any travelers who had been there and our guidebook provided minimal information about the town.

A long, four-hour bus ride from Chitwan National Park through beautiful countryside brought us to the little Nepalese city.

Selecting lodging was easy, as there were only two guesthouses in the entire town. On our first full day, we walked around town, focusing on the market area and the many small stores. Most establishments sold fruits, vegetables, clothing, and household items. Westerners were not often seen, and many locals stared at us as we strolled through the winding streets.

Set on the side of rugged mountains, Gorkha was ideal for small-scale trekking. Taking on the Annapurna mountain range would have been too much, but the trails to the tops of the hillsides surrounding Gorkha were perfect.

Purchasing the ingredients for a picnic lunch, we left early on our second full day in town, planning to hike some of the local trails. The amount of rice and vegetable terracing on these incredibly steep hills was astounding. It has always intrigued me that so many different ancient civilizations developed the skill of terracing while being thousands of miles apart from each other. Peru, China, Nepal, and Bali are just a few of the places where we have seen this antiquated skill. Noticing the similarities, I always wonder if there was some form of communication or trade amongst these civilizations.

Our trek took us to the top of a mountain overlooking the city. The view of the local mountains was beautiful, although the Himalayas were obscured by haze. The hilltop had a beautiful temple as well as a garrisoned military station.

Another four-hour bus ride took us to the greater Kathmandu valley. Although a large city of over a million people, we were able to find quaint shops and stores in the midst of heavy traffic and polluted air. In addition to the tourist sites, we found the city to be a window-shopper's paradise, which delighted Christine over much of the next two weeks. Tibetan carpets, Pashmina scarves, Buddhist prayer wheels, and specialized climbing attire are but a few of the many interesting goods for sale in the metropolitan area.

Bhaktapur, an old city about twenty kilometers from Kathmandu, made for an interesting five-day side trip. Winding, narrow alleyways gave it a feeling of antiquity. Nestled within were great temples and nice little eating houses. We were fortunate to be there in the middle of a festival with much food, drink, and amusement. The massive tug of war in Bhaktapur Square was the main focus of the week's activities, as half of the town competed with the other half in this display of strength and coordination. The winning side held court for the next year, which impassioned the competitors, causing tempers to flare. Though our experience was peaceful, there had been an outbreak of violence leading to stone throwing at the same event the previous year. We did notice heavy police presence, though it did not disrupt the pleasure of the moment.

While in Bhaktapur, I happened to read that Sir Edmund Hillary's ascent to Mount Everest actually began in this city. Back in the early 50s, Nepal lacked the roads to transport him and his party to the base of the mountain, so his group made preparations in Bhaktapur. From here, they hiked over a hundred kilometers of trails before even reaching the base of the mountain. Today, mountain climbers have the advantage of better equipment as well as motorized transport to the base of Everest. This is not to minimize the difficulty of the climb itself, but does convey the added challenge of climbing the mountain fifty years ago.

Back in Kathmandu, Christine and I prepared for our flight over Everest by buying a ticket for the 6:30 a.m. flight via Buddha Airline. Due to the haze in the month of March, we had very few clear views of the Himalayan Range. The earliest possible flight was our best bet to get a clear panorama of the mountains.

Arriving at the airport, we were surprised by the intense security Nepal used for a domestic flight. Although we had no luggage, our handbags, pockets, and camera case were all searched and x-rayed before departure.

Ascending rapidly from the Kathmandu valley, we found ourselves in the midst of the Himalayan range within fifteen to twenty minutes. The fourteen-passenger plane was equipped with a row of seven seats on either side of the plane. Each passenger had their own clear window for viewing and photography. A knowledgeable and helpful roving stewardess provided each passenger with a map of the entire range, listing major peaks and points of interest. Flying over Nepalese airspace to the south of the range, we flew parallel to the mountains in a westerly direction, so the passengers on the right side of the plane had an excellent view. The plane then made a U-turn and flew from west to east so the people on the opposite side had optimal viewing.

The skies were a picture-perfect blue and the entire Himalayan range, as well as Mount Everest, was as clear as could be, enabling us to take many photographs for this memorable Christmas present atop the world.

Although most people tend to think of Mount Everest when contemplating the Himalayas, one of the most amazing things, in my opinion, was the multitude of snow-capped peaks that embrace the mountains over hundreds of miles. The view of the entire range over the wing tips of our airplane was divine.

"Merry Christmas," Christine said to me as we exited the plane, a huge grin on her face.

"Merry Christmas." And we hugged and kissed.

The flight over Mount Everest was a truly wonderful Christmas gift.

CHAPTER 53

A Picnic on the Great Wall

Beijing was our last stop on our thirty-day trip through China. We had begun in Canton in the south, and worked our way north through some of the more prominent cities and sites.

We waited to decide from which location we should view the Great Wall. Having seen photographs from multitudes of people that visited the Badaling site, we were looking for something more enticing.

"The most visited attraction in China has to be approached with caution," remarked Christine.

"Yes, I remember Lu warned us about crowds at Badaling. What was the name of the place he suggested?"

"I forget exactly, but I have it marked on the map he gave us," Christine said. Looking it over, she continued, "Here it is: Simatai."

"It looks much further from Beijing than Badaling."

"He said it would be further away and more difficult to reach, but also that it was worth the extra effort."

"Why don't we ask at the hotel? Maybe they can arrange something other than public buses," I suggested.

That evening, we read about Simatai, and found that it was one hundred ten kilometers from Beijing. The daunting element that keeps tourists away was not the distance from

Beijing, but that it is a very mountainous area and involves some steep climbing.

"Do you still want to try it?" my wife asked.

"I want to make the most of this opportunity, which I think involves going to Simatai," I responded immediately.

The hotel attendant informed us that he could have a minivan pick us up on the morning after next, for a reasonable price. He also added that it was a three-hour trip, in one direction.

Looking at me, Christine nodded. "Let's do it."

Concurring with her, we immediately signed up for the round-trip transportation.

On the morning of departure, we were a bit chagrined to find the van already had six other passengers. I looked at Christine and pessimistically said, "There will probably be thousands of people at Simatai, if our van is full at seven in the morning."

"We'll just have to make the most of it," she responded.

After a three-hour drive, we entered an empty parking lot at our destination.

"We must be the first here," I commented.

We began our walk toward the wall. The views from below were undulating, as we could see the Great Wall traversing the line of mountains.

"Look over there." I pointed. "It looks like there's a gondola going up the mountain." We proceeded toward the base of the hillside. "It goes half way up the mountain. Let's hop aboard."

"No lines either," Christine noted.

The climb up the mountain, beyond the gondola, was very steep, as the book had mentioned. However, we were at the summit within half an hour.

The Great Wall, at this location, has only been partially rebuilt, so hiking along the top is probably like it would have been a hundred years ago.

"Aged with grace, and not yet modernized," I reflected.

There were walls within walls and places where the drop-off was in excess of a hundred feet. Every five hundred feet, there were the remains of guard towers and living quarters for the soldiers of that bygone era. The hike along the wall was steep at times, and not for the faint-hearted, but certainly worth the effort.

With a great view from the top of one of the ramparts, we enjoyed our picnic lunch, sitting on the Great Wall of China. With time to spare and binoculars and camera in hand, we relished the moment.

Breaking out a Coke and cold coffee, we made a toast to our son, Sean. It was his thirty-second birthday.

Even atop the Great Wall, in this less popular section, vendors are hard to avoid. Scurrying among the debris, a post card saleswoman found a rusted nail which she stated was from a wood superstructure that once housed soldiers. Since we purchased post cards from her, she gave us the nail. We still have it in our collection of artifacts from around the world, though we are somewhat skeptical of its origins.

"Who knows?" I commented to Christine, after the lady had left us.

Looking with the binoculars at the parking lot below, I noticed that not another vehicle had parked there since our arrival. We had in fact only seen eight tourists all day, including ourselves.

"What a day!" Christine exclaimed as we hugged each other.

We spent a total of four hours on the Wall before returning to the van and then back to Beijing.

It appeared as though the Chinese government had built the infrastructure at Simatai for masses of tourists that never made it this far out. In addition to the large parking lot and cable car, there were restaurants and a hotel, all of which were empty.

It had been another great day in the annals of our travels. Once again, our extra effort had paid off handsomely. We had enjoyed one of the treasures of the world and would recommend Simatai to any hardy soul.

The Beijing area has many great things to offer travelers. During our brief stay of five days, we picnicked at the Forbidden City, the Summer Palace, and the Great Wall, in addition to enjoying lesser sights and taking in many of the city's markets. It was a perfect conclusion to our stay in China.

CHAPTER 54

An Apartment in Thailand

Now in our seventh year without a place to hang our hat, we pledged to find a suitable location in Southeast Asia. Saigon, Vientiane, and Bangkok were the main contenders. In all of those locations, I would be able to teach part-time, do some painting, and we would have access to limited English libraries. Most important was that all of these places had international airports, which gave us access to the world for continued travel.

"Vientiane is a nice, slow-paced city," I remarked.

"Yes, but it may have its cultural limitations with such a small population base," my wife responded.

"It does have an airport, but we would have to fly to Bangkok before setting off for other places."

"You're right, and Saigon would have the same limitation, although it is a much larger city and will have a broader cultural selection," she added.

"Air pollution is another problem Saigon has. Remember the couple we met in Honduras who had developed breathing problems after living six months in Saigon?"

"Bangkok has air problems also," Christine stated, "but it does have a lot of things going on culturally—and we can fly direct to many places in the world."

"We're flying into Bangkok. Why not stick around a while and see what we can find for apartments?" I suggested.

"Sounds good to me," Christine agreed.

After finding temporary budget housing in Bangkok, we proceeded to seek out cultural activities, English libraries, and apartments. The Bangkok Post and the tourist bureau were helpful tools for locating libraries and cultural activities, but our search for an apartment was futile. In addition to the pollution problem, we discovered that ease of transportation was very important. On one occasion, we located a nice apartment at a reasonable cost, only to find it took us two hours by bus to drive the four kilometers to the sky train system. Housing within walking distance of the sky train was more expensive than many stateside apartments. With ready access to water taxis, riverside apartments were also very expensive.

Then one day, as I happened in the tourist office, the director of tourism was present. He spoke excellent English. I engaged in a lengthy conversation about apartments in and around Bangkok. Using a map, he circled a number of areas with apartments, going over the pros and cons of each.

Then all of a sudden, he looked at me and said, "I have an idea. Take the water taxi north, to the very end of the line. That will bring you to Nonthaburi. Take a look around there."

"What's the town like?" I asked.

"It's very Thai, which also means the prices will be very reasonable," he responded.

The next day, we took a thirty-minute boat ride north to Nonthaburi. We did indeed find it to be very Thai, as the director had stated.

Over the next several hours, we walked the streets, market area, and scouted apartments, all without seeing a single westerner. That in itself was a plus in our minds, in that we had no desire to live in an expatriate enclave. We like Thai people very much and are fond of their culture.

Access to the big city via water taxi was also a big plus. We enjoyed river transportation and the air over the river was much more breathable than on the city streets.

On a subsequent trip upriver, we located an apartment overlooking the river. It was a Thai-style apartment, which is one large room that encompasses the entire flat, with the addition of a bathroom. Being seven stories up, there were nice views, as well as cleaner air.

At this point, we began to feel some anxiety, thinking about the location and the fact that it meant a considerable change in lifestyle. Henceforth, instead of traveling nine or ten months of the year, we would be headquartered in Thailand's capital. We planned to take thirty to sixty-day travel trips from there, hopefully two or three times each year. After six years of travel, we knew we had to slow down, for life in perpetual motion was taking its toll. However, changing lifestyles was easier to say than do. Additionally, there were still so many places to see, and this would certainly slow our pace.

"I have an idea," Christine stated enthusiastically. "Let's take a two-month trip to Indonesia and use the time to think this over."

"That's a great idea," I exclaimed, "We have to leave Thailand anyway, to renew our visas."

The sixty-day trip to Indonesia ended up being a four-month journey, as we added the Malay Peninsula and Borneo to our agenda. This gave us ample time to reflect on the idea of settling in Bangkok.

We slowly acknowledged that Bangkok was a good choice for our purposes. Thus, when returning to Thailand, we stopped via Penang, Malaysia, to obtain one-year visas for Thailand.

With the necessary documents in hand, we proceeded earnestly in our search for a place of residence.

Many of our conversations brought us back to the place overlooking the river in Nonthaburi.

"Why don't we take a boat north tomorrow, and see if we can negotiate a reasonable lease?" Christine suggested.

The next day, we agreed on terms for a one-year lease with the owner of the building. On the subsequent day, we moved in. It happened quite quickly, as we only had three pieces of luggage. The apartment included a bed and dresser, with the bathroom having a commode, sink, and cold-water shower.

The following two or three weeks, we felt like twenty-something-year-old newlyweds, planning and buying items for our new apartment. It was a lot of fun.

With about one hundred square meters of open space, we had much to do. Our number one priority was the kitchen. The newly-leased flat did not have a kitchen sink. With our willing landlord handling the plumbing, we soon had a semi-equipped kitchen and hot-water shower. In time, we added a television, desk, sofa, bookshelves, and an aviary.

Everything worked out marvelously. The original apartment we had looked at was occupied, so to our benefit, we ended up with a front apartment, directly over the water. Fifty percent of our wall space was windows, which provided us with a terrific view. On New Year's Eve and the King and Queen's birthdays, we had an excellent vantage point to observe the fireworks of ten to fifteen different communities.

The nearby market provided Christine with an abundance of very inexpensive ingredients for meal prep. Once again, I felt blessed to be married to such an outstanding cook.

Art shows, a movie festival, music recitals, and a good English library all helped to keep us entertained.

We continued to travel, though on a less exhausting schedule. Last fall, we spent a month in China, followed by a month in South Korea. We have just returned from a week at an island in the Gulf of Thailand and will be off to Vientiane for a week at the end of this month. Our tentative plans for later this year have us taking a trip to Tibet, Nepal, and Bhutan. Subsequent years will hopefully see us in Egypt, southern Africa, Sri Lanka, the Philippines, and possibly a journey on the Trans-Siberian Railway.

Every time we meet a traveler who has been to sites we have not been, we seem to add to our hope-to-go-to list. The world is a bigger place than many people imagine. There are so many places and things to see and do. As long as our health holds up, we intend to see as many as possible.

CHAPTER 55

How We Did It

"How did you manage to retire at fifty-two and do all that traveling?" Patrick asked.

Before I could respond to the question, his wife Alice interjected, "That's the life we would like to live."

The most frequently asked question that Christine and I are confronted with is: How did you do it?

People from all walks of life are curious about how we managed to change our lives so dramatically. Young backpackers are surprised that we could give up a fixed home life. Middle-agers want to get off the treadmill, but doubt that they can before reaching full retirement age.

Years ago, Christine and I asked ourselves what we most wanted to do with the remaining years of our lives.

Although in our mid-forties when we asked the question, it is one that perhaps everyone should ask themselves periodically. For us, the answer was simple. We both wanted to travel and see the world. At that time, we had various commitments which kept us working most of the year, so we set up a long-term plan which would provide us, little by little, with more time. The real key to inexpensive travel is time. The more time, the easier it is to wander the world within a budget.

We suspected that we could live more simply and inexpensively than we had in our previous years. We learned over the next few years that we could travel for less money than it costs to live in the United States. At that point, we began extensive planning and made necessary changes in order to implement this major shift in life.

We lived in an apartment at that time. We had sold our house in upstate New York four years earlier, when our son had graduated from college. About half of our furniture had been given to him upon selling our home, and the remainder was used to furnish our four-room apartment in Charleston, South Carolina.

To embark on our seven years of near perpetual travel, we gave up our apartment and sold nearly all of our furnishings. We rented a ten-by-ten-foot storage space which housed our remaining personal items and a few electronics.

Our second undertaking was to dismantle portions of our business, while keeping enough of it to support our travel plans. We had developed a small business, which proved to be quite seasonal. This was a blessing in disguise, as we could whittle the business down, operating it for a few months each year. Our business expenses were reduced, and we cut our living costs dramatically. We eliminated many things we had taken for granted for years. We found that we could reduce or entirely do away with costly items such as insurance, telephone lines, internet service, and health care. Dental work overseas, for example, is much cheaper than in the United States. One year, Christine needed a tooth crowned. While the dentist in Charleston was much less expensive than his Boston counterpart, we were able to have the crown work done in Oaxaca for one-sixth the South Carolina price. The excellent work was done by a couple who had trained in

California. Countless similar experiences with medical care made it less worrisome to have a catastrophic, high-deductible health insurance plan. (Otherwise, we could be spending more each year on health insurance than on lodging, planes, buses, trains, and boats combined).

Probably the most difficult part of making this dramatic change in our lives involved mental attitude and preparedness. It is not easy to sell off nearly all of your possessions and give up your residence. However, we had the desire, confidence, and knowledge to make low-cost travel our new life. We knew from experience that it could be done. It was more a matter of the details involved in how to do it.

One of the most challenging aspects of our travel was going seven years without a permanent residence. We were on the move, except for when we rented a furnished apartment or set up at a beach for a month or two. Even while working in the States, we would stay in budget motels at monthly rates. Non-residence was the most difficult part of our undertaking. We became essentially homeless. Luckily, we had found an extremely helpful service, run by a couple retired from the military. They received our mail, then sent us an email list showing what personal mail and bills we received. They were authorized to pay the bills on our say-so and periodically would forward mail to us. With this service, we could be homeless without the awkwardness that it represents.

Being travelers also meant that during our time in the States, we had a flurry of activity to prepare for our upcoming absence. Taxes had to be planned, birthday cards purchased, business tax return forms obtained, bills anticipated—all in preparation for the following year. A shopping blitz for items that are better purchased in the States became an annual event. Vitamins and some over-the-counter medicines, Chapstick, and razorblades are on our list. Other must-buys vary according to where we are planning to travel.

After years of being constantly on the move, we were relieved to have a permanent apartment in Bangkok. It provided us a place to return to from our travels. We recently came back from a one-month sojourn to China and it was nice to settle back, read, paint, and enjoy some of Bangkok's cultural events. It is ironic that our form of travel, which sounds so relaxing to other people, is actually very tiring. It is important to take time to relax in between escapades.

We could not have traveled as broadly as we have without low-cost food, lodging, and transportation. Younger backpackers are surprised that we enjoy rough travel. Each of us, in our earlier lives before we knew one another, had traveled quite luxuriously on business and pleasure. Having had those experiences, we do not wish to repeat them, and so do not miss the softer side of travel. For us, it is an advantage to travel without the insulating and isolating comforts of international hotels and tourist packages.

For low-cost food while on the road, we often eat street food, usually choosing the vegetarian selections. Other travelers are often helpful with recommendations. We have read guidebook suggestions for low-cost restaurants, but find that although the books aim to suggest inexpensive, local places, the establishments listed in the books know it, and often, the result is that quality goes down and prices go up. Critical to budget eating is consuming local foods at restaurants frequented by natives. Western style restaurants in third-world countries are always more expensive than local eateries. Balinese people, for example, eat in small diners called *warungs*. These places generally serve good, healthy meals for a dollar or less. If one wants to travel inexpensively, it is necessary to eat at places like that, though it is nice to occasionally splurge on special occasions. When renting furnished apartments, we always take advantage of having a kitchen, if there is one. Usually, home-cooking costs less than eating in restaurants.

Guidebooks and fellow travelers have been very useful in helping us locate inexpensive lodging. Although rates vary from one country to another, we usually attempt to maintain a ten-dollar per night limit for guesthouses and hotels. Though that is near impossible in places like Australia, it is feasible in Central and South America, as well as much of Asia. During our visit to Australia, we nearly always stayed in backpacker lodges that were over our ten-dollar limit, but they usually had kitchen facilities, which enabled us to save on food. This helped balance our budget on that particular trip. In India, we routinely had two-dollar rooms, which offset more expensive destinations on that year's circuit. These rooms are not fancy, but they do offer a bed with an adequate mattress, toilet, and shower (often cold water but not a problem in ninety-degree weather), and sometimes breakfast.

We rarely book a room in advance, preferring to head for the area we have chosen, then look around. One of us stays with our luggage in a coffee shop or park bench, while the other checks out beds, room rates, and other essentials in the guesthouse choice.

Transportation needs to be divided between local transport within a nation and transportation to and from countries.

We use consolidators for trans-Pacific and multi-stop plane tickets. We generally find them to have lower airfares than most travel agencies or airline websites. Once tickets have been purchased, it is important to stick to the schedule as much as possible, as changes usually cost money. Flexibility is also important in maintaining a budget. Prime time flights prior to Christmas are much more expensive than flying in mid-January, for example.

We keep a close eye on budget airline schedules and fees. Getting on a new route of a budget carrier can be very reasonable. We are flying to Singapore next week, for twenty-five dollars round trip, excluding taxes and airport fees. Christine reserved the flights for us, via the internet, on the first day they were announced. Flexibility was critical as we are flying at their convenience, not ours.

Generally, it is less expensive to travel locally by bus or train than it is to fly. Trains, buses, and long-distance ferries also give different perspectives on a country, concerning not only the scenery, villages, and towns, but also the people and ways in which they travel. Most of our local travel has been by bus, while trains have been more comfortable, and at times, less expensive in China, India, and Thailand. Each country seems to be unique regarding travel, so what works at one place may not work at the next. Mexico probably has one of the most developed and efficient bus systems in the world, while neighboring Belize has a very cumbersome bus operation on horrible roads.

We often carry food with us while traveling on buses or trains. The cleanliness of food at many of the layovers is questionable. It can be tedious eating only bread, bananas, or plain white rice on twelve or twenty-four-hour routes, but it beats Montezuma's revenge.

When going to and from airports, you can often save a considerable amount of money by using the same mode of transportation that airport employees utilize to get to and from work. We reduced our transportation cost at one airport into the city, from twenty dollars to one dollar, by using the local bus. We have also found that some backpacker lodges offer free pickup from airports.

When arriving at a city, we always purchase the local newspaper to see what's going on, in addition to reading the news. We often find concerts, piano recitals, and the like with free admission. On one occasion, we found an all-day tour of temples for a mere two dollars. We were the only westerners to join, and found ourselves welcomed by the locals. The same tour offered by a tourist office costs forty dollars.

Our travel adventures often involve compromises and sacrifices, as do many things in life. One has to have a strong desire and proper mental attitude to undertake seven years of continual travel. We have thoroughly enjoyed our experiences and perhaps our travels have, as a writer we admire said, "stretched the borders of our own lives." We have been moved by the beauty, magnificence, or wondrous origins of many of the great sites of the world. Discomforts pale in contrast with those experiences. We have become vastly aware of the very different lives of the people who inhabit our planet.

There are still many places we want to see and we intend to continue our travels. What we have seen has only whet our appetite for more.

So, how did we do it? We decided to do it—and the rest fell into place.

AFTERWORD

By Sean and Susan Boudreau

Always one to keep busy with hobbies, we can imagine Dad, under a palapa, enjoying the reflective nature of transforming his collection of extraordinary experiences into written word—undoubtedly sharing and hashing out the details with his travel companion and the love of his life, Christine.

We only saw them once or twice per year, so the time together was treasured. They were constantly encountering new and interesting parts of our magnificent world but were more interested in hearing about our everyday lives. Always excellent listeners, they encouraged us in our pursuits in life, rather than talking in much depth about their travels. Hence, we feel fortunate that they provided us with this legacy, though only a glimpse of their adventurous lives.

Following, is an image of their world map, pinpointing places they have journeyed, along with yearly lists showing the progression of their travels. Annual visits with family are not included.

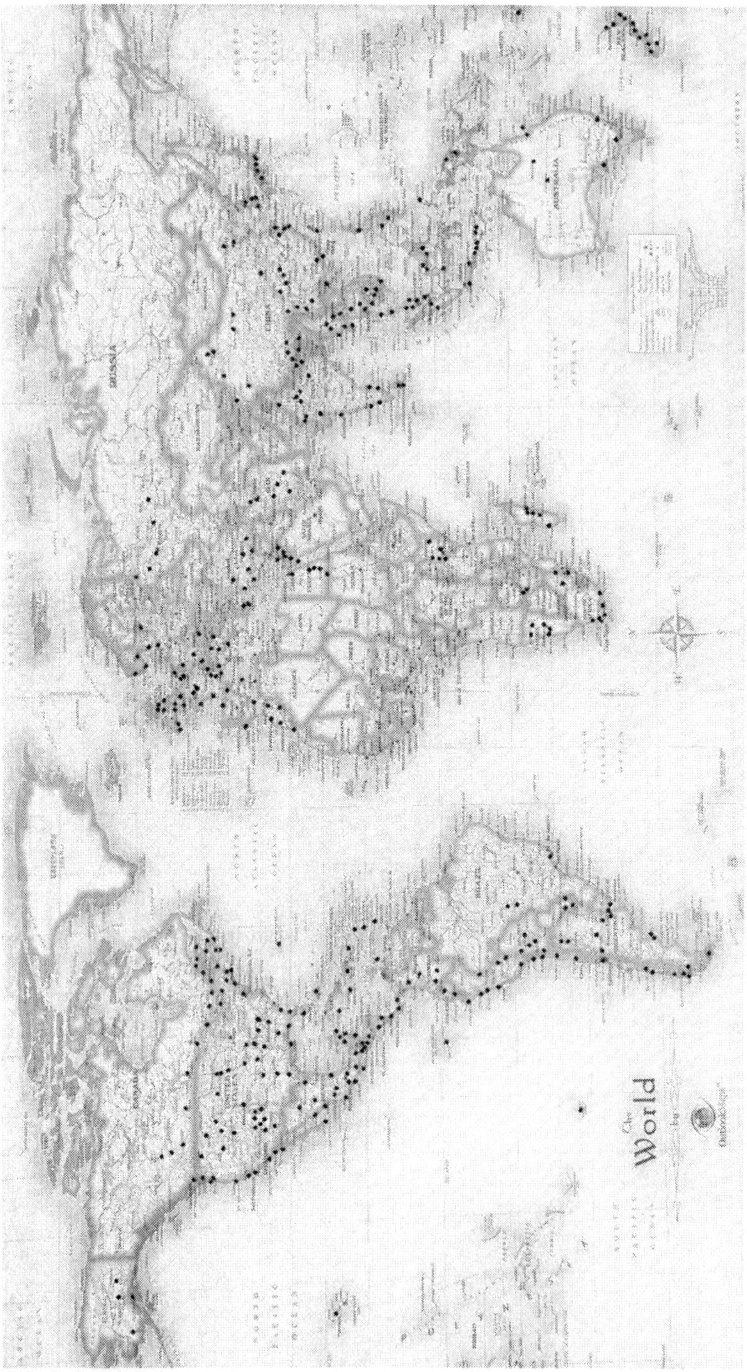
The World

YEARS OF TRAVEL

1995
Mexico - Cancun, Cozumel

1996
Mexico (5 weeks) - Cancun, Playa del Carmen, Paamul, Merida, Oaxaca, Puerto Angel, Puerto Escondido, Taxco, Mexico City

1997
Mexico (9 weeks) - Oaxaca, San Cristobal del las Casas, Puerto Angel, Puerto Escondido, Barra de Potosi, Taxco, Guadalajara, Patzcuaro, Barra Navidad

1998
Mexico (Van for 7 months) - Butterflies in Morelia, Taxco, Barra de Potosi, San Agustinillo, Acapulco, Patzcuaro, Oaxaca, Veracruz
Guatemala - Tikal, Lake Atitlan
Antigua

1999

China - Hong Kong
Thailand - Bangkok, Chiang Mai
Malaysia
Singapore
Indonesia - Bali, Lombok
Australia
New Zealand
Figi
Mexico - Oaxaca

2000

Panama
Costa Rica
Nicaragua
Honduras
Belize
Guatemala
Mexico

2001

England

Bahrein

India

Nepal

Bangladesh

Myanmar (Burma)

Thailand

Cambodia

Vietnam

Laos

Indonesia - Bali, Lombok

China - Hong Kong

2002

Guatemala

Antigua

Costa Rica

Nicaragua

El Salvador

Peru

Bolivia

Ecuador

Galapagos Islands

Mexico - San Agustinillo, Taxco

2003

Thailand - Bangkok

Malaysia - Sarawak

Indonesia - Kalimantan, Java (Borobudur), Bali, Flores

China - Xian, Yangshuo, Guangzhou, Yangtze, Beijing

South Korea

2004

Thailand - Bangkok, Koh Mak

Laos - Vientiane

China - Hong Kong, Hangzhou, Putuoshan, Shanghai, Suzhou, Weitang, Guangzhou, Chengdu, Leshan, Tibet, Lhasa, Shigatse, Gyantse, Sakya, Mount Everest

Singapore

Nepal - Kathmandu, Bhaktapur

Bhutan - Paro, Bumthang, Thimpu

2005

Thailand - Bangkok, Phuket

China - Yunnan, Kunming, Dali, Lijiang, Macao, Tiger Leaping Gorge, Zhongdian, Tengchong, Jomtien Beach, Sabah, Hong Kong

Egypt - Cairo, Aswan, Luxor, Dendera, Sharm El-Sheikh

England - Devon, Preston, London

Kenya

2006
Thailand - Koh Mak

Myanmar (Burma) - Yangon, Ngapali, Bago

China - Chengdu, Urumqi, Hotan, Kashgar, Subashi/Kuche, Turpan, Dunhuang, Shanghai, Hangzhou

Indonesia - Sulawesi, Bali

Japan - Kyoto, Nara

2007
Philippines - Apo, Siquijor

Malaysia - Perhentian

Russia - St. Petersburg, Moscow, Suzdal

New Zealand

2008
Chili - Easter Island

Patagonia

Tierra del Fuego

Argentina - Buenos Aires, Mendoza

Uruguay

Mexico – Oaxaca

2009
Mexico - Yucatan

U.S. - New Orleans, Mount Rushmore

Canada - Rockies to Ottawa, Montreal, Quebec, Maritimes

2010

Madagascar
England
Italy - Rome, Florence, Venice
Columbia
Ecuador
Peru

2011

China - Hong Kong
Thailand - Bangkok
Indonesia - Sumatra, Bali, Gili
New Guinea
Peru - Amazon, Tambopata
Argentina - Salta, Cafayate

2012

Israel
Jordan
Turkey
Brazil - Pantanal
Argentina - Iguazu, Valdes Peninsula
Paraguay
U.S. - Washington DC

2013
U.S. - Florida Keys, National Parks (Zion, Bryce, Grand Canyon)
South Africa
Namibia
Zambia
Zimbabwe
Swaziland

2014
China - Hong Kong
Thailand - Bangkok
India - Rajasthan
Sri Lanka
Turkey
Iran

2015
Morocco
England
Chile - Santiago, Chiloe
Argentina - Mendoza

2016
Canada - Montreal, Quebec, Maritimes
U.S. - Alaska
France (Southern)

2017
U.S. - San Francisco
Peru - Cusco, Machu Picchu, Ayacucho, Lima
France - Gers, Aix-en-Province, Dijon, Lyon

2018
Guatemala
Canada - Prince Edward Island
France - Paris, LaRochelle, Bordeaux, Lascaux, Lasseran

2019
Singapore
China - Hong Kong
Taiwan
Spain
Portugal
U.S. - New York City

2020 (Covid)
U.S. - Arkansas (Crystal Bridges)
Cancelled trips: Austria, Romania, Hungary, Prince Edward Island, Maritimes, France

2021
U.S. - Arizona and Utah National Parks, Eastern Shores and Outer Banks, Austin, Texas

2022
France - Paris, Rowen, Lagon, Epernay
Canada - Prince Edward Island
U.S. - New England, Eastern Shores
Argentina - Buenos Aires, Mendoza
Italy - Milan, Alba, Torino
Saudi Arabia - Riyadh, Al-Ula, Jeddah, Jubbah

ABOUT THE AUTHOR

Richard grew up in a small New England town, the youngest of three children. At age seventeen, he joined the Marine Corps and served as a forward air-controller in combat. He believed in the benefits of education and earned his doctorate from Boston University. In his early career, he taught high school history, which led to his position as president of Fisher College. Always looking for a new challenge, he later owned several small businesses—from agriculture, to real estate, to seasonal retail. At age fifty-two, he and his wife, Christine, made their dream to see the world a reality. Over the years, they have journeyed throughout sixty countries in six continents.